BIOBLOGS

BIOBLOGS

Résumés
for the
21st Century

MICHAEL HOLLEY SMITH

Collins
An Imprint of HarperCollinsPublishers

HarperCollins books may be purchased for educational, business, or sales promotional use. For information please write: Special Markets Department, HarperCollins Publishers, Inc., 10 East 53rd Street, New York, NY 10022.

FIRST EDITION

Designed by Nancy Singer Olaguera

Library of Congress Cataloging-in-Publication Data

Smith, Michael Holley.
    Bioblogs : résumés for the 21st century / Michael Holley Smith.—1st ed.
      p.cm.
    ISBN-10: 0-06-113039-7
    ISBN-13: 978-0-06-113039-7
    1. Résumés (Employment) 2. Internet advertising. 3. Blogs. I. Title.
    HF5383.S628   2006
    650.14'2028567—dc22   2006040332

10 9 8 7 6 5 4 3 2 1

CONTENTS

INTRODUCTION
BEFORE THEY BLINK

BIOBLOGS ARE DESIGNED TO GRAB ATTENTION BEFORE THE READER HAS A CHANCE TO BLINK. If you can persuade the company's HR representative to take a momentary pause at your bioblog as he or she plows through the daily pile of paper and electronic résumés, or—better yet, if you can maneuver that rep's focus onto a powerful graphic that captures in a flash the image of your creativity (and, thus, your potential value to their corporate mission and endeavors), you have succeeded in the crucial, critical, sudden-death competition of "getting your résumé to stand out."

If the HR rep stops to ponder the *you* in your bioblog when thumbing through the stack of look-alike résumés, you have forged the first link that connects your creative identity to the company's unknown search criteria, which you can safely wager these days is based upon locating an exceptional, innovative, and resourceful individual to hire.

Bioblogs are not for the run-of-the-mill worker with a low range of ambition, performance, or expectations; if you are not a creative character with the keen sense of what's on the leading edge of workplace dynamics (such as the importance of emotional intelligence in team playing), then you are barking up the wrong tree by making yourself out to be different. You have to be willing to take a degree of intellectual risk, to stand behind the argument for your legitimate credentials "as advertised" by the total psychological effect of your bioblog's image and words.

Just as experienced web searchers have learned quickly to separate the credible from the come-ons through the vast clutter of global websites, a savvy HR rep will sense when you are too clever by half in your bioblog, so you have to be honest about what you are promoting when you put your creativity up for sale.

Bioblogging and promoting your personal creativity are one and the same, and that's precisely why they represent an art form whose time has come. Employers recognize the performance value and bottom-line potential to what has heretofore been relegated to second-class passage, the *inherent future creativity* implied in a person's history as roughly sketched in a résumé. Whereas traditional résumé forms have generally accomplished their goals by listing work and education with various styles and flair, today, when some twenty million résumés circulate the World Wide Web daily, those formats are flat and empty. They just don't work well for waving your flag in a sea of banners.

Creativity is the keyword of the twenty-first century. In fact, Columbia Business School now offers a class called Creativity and Personal Mastery, which is becoming popular in B-schools nationwide. (Interestingly, the class is so popular at the London Business School that a vigorous application process must be completed to qualify for the class, including submitting a résumé—a good time to employ a well-crafted bioblog if I ever heard of one.)

For your information, résumés have been around in the same basic form since the 1940s, when they were used exclusively by VIPs and men in high-paying jobs. In the 1960s and '70s, they trickled down to the masses of middle managers that populated most companies in the booming economy; in the '80s and '90s, as the world's segmented markets emerged as global competitors (and personal computers with cheap printers made their way into the mainstream), résumés were cranked out by everyone and their mother (who were reentering the workforce after rearing children at home). Everyone with any work plans at all had a résumé, and that seemed good enough for most folks.

It was, but that was then and this is now, and we're in a different world. Outsourcing and other cost-cutting measures allow companies to save their burgeoning budgets for the best creative performers, relegating more mundane tasks to cheaper labor markets. This is why bioblogs are designed for the cream of the crop. They offer the best chance to make your creative potential stand out. Strum through the one hundred sample bioblogs in this book, and you will quickly recognize why, and will probably think to yourself, after hundreds of hours of combing the Internet: Of course, this is where résumés have to go; this is what's needed.

Now go make one, or make many. Allow yourself to be as creative as you would like to be. You are no longer bound by the restraints of traditional résumés. If you cannot execute technically what you can create conceptually, talk a friend into producing your bioblog for you, or hire someone with expertise in graphic management. However you choose to do it, get it distilled onto paper or a computer screen to your essence—that creative qualifications core of what makes you a better choice for hiring and joining an employer's team.

This book shows everything you need to get ahead of the pack with your bioblog, a brand-new art form. I predict that in less than a decade just about everyone in the top 25 percent of desirable candidates will be bioblogging, because for one reason, it's a lot of fun, and also, it serves to get the message across better than any other résumé form. Until we can create a nanoversion of our applicant selves that can do a dog-and-pony show on somebody's desk, this will be the best we can do.

Remember: *You are the message.* Make it creative and vibrant, desirable beyond mere words, a self-image that points toward your creative future. Bioblogging provides the means to promote your best qualities rather than bore the reader with the monotonous litany of your employers, titles, duties, and underplayed achievements (which invariably seem insignificant without the color of how they happened). Use it as a guide for the personal interview to follow, convincing a prospective employer that your self-awareness, emotional intelligence, resourcefulness, and creativity are worth the price you insist on.

After all, the fact is, *you are selling the future you,* not the past record of who hired you and what you did (or didn't do). Your bioblog is about that future you, the one that, ultimately, potential employers will have to gamble on. Make it easy for them, and for yourself, with a stunning bioblog.

1

SELFWORK

YOU ARE WHO YOU ARE. Let's begin our conversation with that undeniable and subtle given; from there we can go on to examine *the business of your creative character* and what it does for or against you in your work. To accomplish this, we'll review the common links connecting the various aspects of your personality, as well as how effectively they meld in the work "place" (a psychological and social briar patch).

Before we begin, let's also take a moment to establish some essential guiding principles to keep in mind as we investigate and improvise. With regard to your individual character and how well it can succeed at work:

- You will do your most notable work when you engage your best character traits.
- Your best traits will determine how well you will fit in a company's culture and its levels of expectations for your performance.
- Your success in becoming integrated into the company's stated mission will determine how well you can promote your character's particular strengths.
- Your ability to promote *the becoming you* is contingent upon how well you can maintain a realistic, though subjective, sense of self-measurement over time.
- Your successful self-promotion must be confirmed through a company's public recognition/rewards, beginning with authentication by coworkers and peers.

First things first, however, because if you are not already inside a company that is worth all this energy and effort, you must persuade the gatekeepers to a different company to open its door and let you in—at least for a look-see. This is the sole reason why we need to utilize the new art form of bioblogs—to be noticed in order to take further action, to move beyond the initial "cold call" threshold, where you're on the outside, and into the dynamics of the "personal interview," where the rubber meets the road in face-to-face traction and engagement.

The immediate task is to recognize and act on the basis that the most valuable qualities you can possibly offer an employer are those that apply to the widest range of workplace environments: i.e., *the adaptable but true qualities of your creative character.*

For us to determine precisely what this means from the perspective of a potential employer, which is an important first step, let's delve into some of the most obvious facets of "creative character for hire at work" and how the employer sees it.

In simplified terms, any employer that is seeking a qualified worker needs the most direct and unadorned answer to, Do you know what you want and how we fit in this picture? The answer to this question will tell the employer a lot from the start, and part of the professional interviewer's biggest challenge is to distill this difficult, complex issue into an answerable query. What the HR representative will want to know next is, What kind of person are you?

So the employer wants to know right up front: Do you know what you want?

Then it wants to learn if you have figured out whether the company can offer it to you.

Then the employer needs to know if you are the kind of person who can fit in the company culture.

Next comes, Are you this company's kind of person? This is the focal point from then on, and once this loaded question is transformed into a satisfactorily known quantity, the next layer of questions will be to reveal, What can we do with this person's creative character? In other words, if it discerns measurable values in your creative characteristics, it can look beyond the narrow focus of a particular title or work classification to see if there is another area in which you might be more useful; and once it manages this quandary, the rest will be a basic matter of metrics: How much do you want from us?

This is a streamlined version of the elaborate labyrinths through which employers lead candidates, sometimes sensibly and at other times incomprehensibly, even to them. A million different employers may employ thousands of different styles in approaching their particular candidates. For example, as an extreme view, Hewlett Packard's strategy for weeding out applicants is a far cry from the ploys and techniques used by franchises, such as Burger King, or retail stores, such as Dollar General. One size doesn't fit all, except in the sense that strong character traits—such as persistence, honesty, dedication, reliability, focus on the job, desire to do the best work, ability to make decisions independently—are welcomed universally, and are naturally going to be more desirable and more readily rewarded by a manager or supervisor.

The difference begins with the first impression, be it e-mail or snail mail or instant messaging or job posting or web portfolio or any other form. The potential employer's first look at your self-presentation can make or break you. There are no second chances if you fail on the first cut. An applicant who shows up wearing his gimme cap backward is unlikely to receive the same reaction as one who wears a dress shirt and tie; it merely reflects a willingness to put forth an effort to become a viable representative for the company. The message delivered is "I can make you proud and happy" rather than "I'm here to kill hours and get a paycheck."

A bioblog is the best new way to create a good first impression with a prospective employer by conveying powerful images and impressions of your creative capabilities and unique character.

According to Daniel Pink in *A Whole New Mind: Moving from the Information Age to the Conceptual Age,* a major shift is taking place in global business: "The scales are tilting toward right-hemisphere abilities: artistry, empathy and synthesis rather than analysis." And the three forces that are driving this shift are an abundance of consumer goods (leading people to seek both meaning and function from products); outsourcing to Asia (labor flowing to cheaper production); and automation of routine work. What's left requires creative thinking, right-brain stuff—Peter Drucker's "knowledge worker." Because design has become so fundamental to the literacy and form of products and businesses, creating products and services with users in mind is the primary aim now. Some companies are even appointing chief storytelling officers "because story is a form of knowledge management and product differentiation," and meaning is important to workplace stability.

BEING YOUR BEST

Our personality traits are like an expansive coral reef waiting to be explored; we just don't know what's there until we dive in and swim around the underside of these traits to see those parts of ourselves that are not apparent all of the time. Because these traits portray the unfolding dimensions of ourselves and our potential, we have plenty of reasons for putting it all out on a table for dissection.

If we were sick, we would need to figure out why, and devise an action plan to get healthy as soon as possible; if we were confused, we would need to sort out the jigsaw pieces and see what matches and what's missing. If we were unhappy, we would need to intellectually separate our life at home and our life at work to contemplate what's common and what's different, and why there's a troubling conflict, if there is one. And if we were happy, we would need to identify those components of our character that have brought us to this pleasant state, then examine the reasons for greater understanding of ourselves and how we can plan for our future.

In order to discover our relevant traits and plan for our future by becoming a creative high performer at work, our goals should be threefold:

1. to learn who we are
2. to develop our creative character traits
3. to make the most of them in our workplaces

To do this well, we need to concentrate on three primary aspects: (1) whatever it is that makes us feel pleased with ourselves at work when being creative; (2) whatever it is that makes us feel a sense of accomplishment at work when being rewarded for being creative; and (3) whatever it is that makes us feel we are on the right track for our future careers—being introspective and realistic about what we can do with who we are.

If you already believe that your creative character matches your skill sets fairly well, you may already be a creative high performer at work, or one who is definitely in the process of becoming a creative high performer by applying yourself more stringently than those around you. If you are happy or just starting to feel pleasantly content, you have probably abandoned the bad habits of trying to manage the negative behaviors of your past, and have begun to promote yourself with a clear sense of who you are now, and who you may become if you continue on the proper track. You may even have already learned to perceive yourself (for workplace purposes) as a service/product that must have a certain public persona to be fully accepted.

In *You Are the Message,* Roger Ailes, the media mastermind behind the roaring success of the Fox News Channel, says that because what you see is more often than not what you will get, it is crucial that you control your creative character traits as they are seen in the workplace by your peers, managers, and customers; otherwise, the "message" you communicate can conflict with your true creative character. If the two images aren't in sync, you will be working against yourself most of the time. To positively present your creative character, it will serve you well to follow some elementary advice that Ailes and other communication experts suggest, and I add my own counsel from experience, too.

1. Be yourself.

This is probably the most important realization you can make, so it is a great place to start. Trying to be someone other than who you really are is a complete waste of time. Being yourself should be the foundation upon which you build your public persona, the image you present to others in the artificial environment of the workplace, where you must "act" on the "stage" in the "drama" of working with other personalities. As far as character goes, everything you need is already within you; you don't have to beg, borrow, or steal from others. Learn to recognize and respect your own self, whatever it takes.

You have *you* and the whole universe of your own character traits with which to work; that's all you are going to need to succeed, and it's already there for the makings of a great work of art. Not only that, you have your whole life to perfect them. You were born with your natural talents and creative juices, and that's why you are unique, as is everyone else trying to scratch out a living on this hungry planet. There's a lot of folks in the world around you—but there's only one *you*. Your *self* is who you are deep within your own consciousness, not the external image that your peers and coworkers expect of you. Learn to separate *the performing you* from the you who resides inside your sense of peace and acceptance of your character. You don't have to pretend to be someone you aren't, but you do have to oversee your traits like a professional puppet master.

2. Be the centered self that makes you feel sane.

Being centered will sustain you through the cavalcade of confounding difficulties that you will encounter in the routine and unanticipated conflicts inherent in careers and in the workplace. If you can't stand up straight on your own two feet (or sit proudly in your wheelchair), you must get yourself in balance, just as a child must learn how to crawl before trying to walk. Being centered means there is someplace central for your neural pathway energies to gather and feel one for all and all for one. Harmony within the panorama of your creative character traits is a landscape of sanity. You will most certainly know if you are out of balance because you will feel there's something wrong.

Learn to monitor your self for the inner clues, and act quickly to put yourself on stronger footing. This may be a process of getting off the fence of indecision about an issue (e.g., a moral question regarding the right thing to do about a coworker's behavior), and seek good advice to help you take a position and stick with it. Avoid becoming stuck in the mire of "not being sure." Act positively to change or accomplish something; don't just react because you need to; and learn to lead yourself by understanding with certainty what you really believe.

3. Become your best self, the one with the most potential.

That's the lesson from the experts, from Jesus Christ to the Dalai Lama, Margaret Thatcher to Zig Ziglar. Arming yourself with a fortuitous and tenacious tool kit will help you stand up for yourself and what you know and believe. Acting on the potential within, you will bring yourself considerably more happiness than following the crowd: it's not only the best way, it's the only way. Once you have imposed order on the chaos within you, your shining light will burn brighter, illuminating the way for others behind you. Get the best tools and learn how to use them by employing logic over emotion, paying more attention to realistic details than sloppy sketches of ideas.

4. Work like someone is watching you.

It doesn't matter if you are Protestant, Catholic, Muslim, Hindi, or Other—if you are intelligent enough to recognize the grace given to you by your creative spirit, then you are smart enough to realize that you are surely not completely on your own in this world. From my personal experiences, I have always had the feeling that someone was watching me—not so much watching "over" me but watching me from my immediate realm of presence—and it has served to keep me on my toes, constantly trying to do the best job simply to meet my own standards. People notice, believe me.

SAVVY EMOTING

Daniel Goleman, in his book *Working with Emotional Intelligence,* says the newest approach to high performers has "little to do with what we were told was important in school; academic abilities are largely irrelevant of this standard." From this perspective, today's employers take it for granted that a candidate has sufficiently researched a company and its opportunities, and has the intellectual ability and technical know-how to do what is required, at least as far as can be determined in advance of an interview. That part should be a no-brainer.

What should animate you is today's heightened spotlight on a potential employee's "personal qualities, such as initiative and empathy, adaptability and persuasiveness." This is a more discerning direction taken by companies these days and is "no passing fad." In Goleman's research, he reviewed studies of tens of thousands of working people, in callings of every kind, that plainly show with "unprecedented precision which qualities mark a star performer." These studies lead to a general conclusion: the human abilities and capabilities that we understand as those that compose *a person's character are the essential components for excellence in the workplace,* and particularly for leadership.

Goleman found that those who work in large organizations are probably already being evaluated in terms of these human capabilities, though they may not know it, and "if you are applying for a job, you are likely to be scrutinized through this lens, though, again, no one will tell you so explicitly." He makes it clear what most of us have already learned from our experiences in our varied workplaces—that no matter what you do, at any level of work, understanding "how to cultivate these capabilities can be essential for success in your career."

Even if you work for a small company, or have your own business, becoming adept at managing your *emotional intelligence* will to a significant degree determine how successful you are. This is something we creative souls should recognize instantly from our vast work-world experiences, where a levelheaded demeanor can be worth a gold mine. "Almost certainly you were never taught [these people skills] in school," Goleman reflects. "Even so, your career will depend, to a greater or lesser extent, on how well you have mastered these capacities. In a time with no guarantees of job security, when the very concept of a 'job' is rapidly being replaced by 'portable skills,' these are prime qualities that make and keep us employable."

Is he saying that in the world of tomorrow's workers, we are going to become "portable people" with *a personal skills portfolio* formed around the shell of our emotional character and intuitive intelligence? Whew! I haven't seen *that* in the classifieds lately! Richard Florida sums this up in *The Flight of the Creative Class: The New Global Competition for Talent:* "I call the age we are entering *the creative age* because the key factor propelling us forward is the rise of creativity as the prime mover of our economy. Not just technology or information, but human creativity. . . . Perhaps the most incredible thing about the creative age is that it holds the possibility not only for economic growth and prosperity, but also for a much fuller development of human potential in general . . . people love to do creative work; it's what we're about" and "more people than ever before are getting to do creative work for a living." Workers must harness and understand their creative character and emotional intelligence skills in order to leverage them when seeking a new job.

CREATIVE CHARACTER AT WORK

Creative character at work is what we're talking about: resourceful, creative people who are "in touch with themselves," who will be the leaders of tomorrow, if they aren't already today, such as gamers who have become CEOs of fast-growing companies. We must promote ourselves for these choice jobs; we need to address head-on the essential questions relating to the survival, growth, and longevity of our careering throughout the promotion of our creative character traits; and we must never stop asking ourselves the right questions. Nor can we allow ourselves to become complacent with our position and worldview. Change will overtake us if we do not maintain an eye for self-vigilance, being aware of our needs to adapt as the world around us changes.

Ask yourself these questions in order to develop an ongoing plan for fine-tuning your creative character traits in your current workplace and for future employers:

- What immediate future event will have the greatest impact on my creative character?
- What will happen to my creative character as my career progresses?
- What can I do now to strengthen my self for the future?

We can also convert this to a job-search strategy in order to tailor our strongest character traits to the specific targets of our queries and search activities. For this purpose, these questions become:

- What kind of future can my target company offer me and my creative character?
- What will the actual workplace be like for my individual personality traits?
- What can I do now to get a potential employer to realize the benefits of my creative character?

Again, it is crucial to understand the process of a "meeting of the minds" (creative characters intermeshing: yours and theirs) from their perspective, which is the one that will be the deciding factor. By subverting your needs to theirs, and by tailoring your creative character traits to what they really want, you can prevent a substantial amount of anxiety from the onset.

A CALL FOR THE NEW CREATIVITY

Creative people in American society stand out in part because the large percentage of an unmotivated workforce tends to believe in a Father State that will make everything right, eliminate social inequities, and protect a collectivist "public good." Our modern government-financed educational system has undervalued personal performance for the sake of the welfare of others. It is a place where self-esteem is instilled for the purpose of social equality. It has, unfortunately, concocted an unreal bubble out of which creative thinkers, through willful independence and self-promotion, must burst. They must assert that there is no insurance policy against absolutely everything, and argue that Big Government cannot initiate a national policy to make everyone behave well, act properly, or be inspired and creative. We as individuals must learn to stand up for individuals.

A sense of complacency permeates many workplaces in our times, and it can affect our economic future in the worst way. (India and China have taken note, to be sure.) Educational crusader Alfie Kohn warns us that the "progressive" educational approaches currently in vogue, relying heavily on standardized curricula and testing, actually hinder the learning process. Alan J. Rowe, in *Creative Intelligence: Discovering the Innovative Potential in Ourselves and Others,* says, "A significant problem confronting our educational system is the orientation toward preparing students for a single career," although we (experts and workplace observers) have long known that the reality is "most people have multiple careers during their working lives."

This "multiple careers" factor is something I have witnessed in my thousands of interviews while helping my clients try to explain (often apologize for) their checkerboard career paths—why they were one thing (accounting assistant) and then another (office manager) and then later yet another (marketing rep) and now looking for still another (sales manager). What drove me crazy was continually trying to assuage a client's fears that his history was not as unusual, atypical, or somehow different as he suspected. In fact, probably fewer than 20 percent of my clients enjoyed a straight-line career path from a college degree to the job they ended up taking (often because they "knew someone who knew someone").

Not only that, with my college-educated clients, an astonishing number of them didn't work in the field in which they earned their degree, and most of them seemed to believe that "having a degree" (in anything) was what made it worth it, not the specialized knowledge that allegedly came with a specific course of study. I was often amused by people who had spent years (four, five, six) earning bachelor's degrees—in biology or social work or political science—who then ended up finding work in marketing or sales, or people with a degree in marketing who end up as bartenders and restaurant managers. (In fact, I would bet if you asked your spouse/lover/best friend and peers about their work histories, theirs, too, will be dotted with these perceived incongruities, which are actually the norm as far as I can tell.) The grid that is supposed to line up "what you want to do" with "what you end up doing" is packed full of holes, most of them big enough to drive a truck through.

SCRAMBLED MATRIX

The matrix of *what you do* lining up with *who you are* seems hopelessly scrambled. Richard Florida's analysis pierces right into the cortex of the opportunities with which we must figure out what to do:

*   *   *

One of the greatest fallacies of modern times is that creativity is limited to a small group of people with particular talents. Most people, the belief goes, don't want to be creative, couldn't do it if asked, and would be very uncomfortable in an environment where creativity was expected of them. This belief is false.

The single most overlooked—and single most important—element of my theory is the idea that every human being is creative. By our very nature, each and every person is endowed with an incredible capacity for innovation, a by-product of the innate human capability to evolve and adapt. Creative capital is thus a virtually limitless resource.

His humanism fits neatly with my strategy for promoting creative character at work; it maintains that each of us has "creative potential that we strive to exercise, and that can be turned to valuable ends," and that if we are going to prosper as individuals and as a society, "we can no longer tap and reward the creative talents of a minority; everyone's creative capabilities must be fully engaged."

Being ahead of the pack is a good thing, and you don't need to look back; you don't learn much by seeing who is following you.

We are in danger of heading the wrong way down a one-way interstate highway, and we had better turn around soon if we are going to avoid a head-on collision with our global competition. Florida writes, "The United States today faces its greatest competitive challenge of the past century, perhaps of its young life. The reason is basic: The key factor of the global economy is no longer goods, services, or flows of capital, but the competition for people. The ability to attract people is a dynamic and sensitive process. New centers of the global creative economy can emerge quickly; established players can lose position. It's a wide-open game, and the playing field is leveling every day."

A GAMBLE

We've been gambling our careers on the wrong cards, ones we've had in our hands but not in our hearts, a random collection of mismatched jobs and skills of a kind. For years we've known intuitively, perceived directly from our very own tactile experiences with all kinds of characters in the workplaces in which we've learned, but it's only been recently that we have begun to whisper among ourselves, and admit that:

To a stranger (who is another worker, by the way) who must determine who we really are, we are a numbered enigma wrapped in a blanket of unknowns, an e-mailed file, a name scrawled on a manila folder, a no-name person who's posted on a web portfolio. He or she must begin by knowing absolutely nothing—less than zero, really—about us. The HR representative is not just starting from scratch (which would be zero), because he or she has prejudices and preferences and discriminating guidelines to impose at the very beginning of the process. The rep may not like or want people with names ending in a vowel, may not like or need people with unrelated experiences, may not want or like people from a certain geographical area, may not want people who question his or her ability to question them!

There are thousands of these mutable elements. Historically, in the two hundred years of American commercial enterprises and associated hiring-and-firing activities, in the typical processes of careering, the critical mass of one's marketability has leaned toward what one did, and that has been what we have been judged by.

It doesn't have to always be that way.

We need to change that embedded form in the minds of interviewers/screeners; we need to divert it to the matter of who creative workers are and what we want, not what we've done.

And for this, we need bioblogs.

BEST BAIT CATCHES EMPLOYERS' ATTENTION

The basic concept of bioblogs is to make the strongest, best impression on an HR representative as quickly as possible—in the very first glance. Bioblogs are not only "best practices," they're "best bait." They should provoke a nibble at first sight, then, like all bait used by professional fishermen and -women, they should be delectably noticeable while simultaneously acceptably innocuous—i.e., the fish shouldn't be wary of it just because it looks so good, but it should look so good that it'll attract attention. What you are doing is making your bait attractive to HR by saying, "Look at me! I'm creative! I have more potential! I'm selling the value of my Now, not the record of my past!"

By accentuating the positives of creative character from the get-go, you can disarm some of the routine negative barriers, and you will activate the start-up phase of a more involved engagement with a hiring entity—headhunter, search firm, recruiter, screener, personal contact—that will bode well for you from the very beginning.

Impress the rep from the first contact, follow up with a self-confident understanding of your self, deliver your presentation with assuring and persuasive body language, and provide key details and requested information in the most emotionally intelligent manner.

Your ultimate strategy is first to defuse any negative prejudices of a first impression, and you'll do this with a powerful bioblog that presents you well. Since no résumé in any form can answer all of the questions (appropriately or otherwise), we are not concerned with that; instead, what we want to achieve is enough force of persuasion in the design and content of our bioblog that we put a positive light on any relevant aspects of the following issues—issues that an employer has on its short list of "things to figure out about you."

> Can the creative character of this potential employee be put to a use other than what he or she is applying for?
>
> Can the creative character of this potential employee be altered in any way for a better fit with one of our teams?
>
> Can the creative character of this potential employee make better use of coworkers' time, talents, and energies?
>
> Can the creative character of this potential employee improve operations, service, or product quality?
>
> Can the creative character of this potential employee raise the bar for customer response and satisfaction?
>
> Can the creative character of this potential employee cut waste or unnecessary work, or do it faster?
>
> Can the creative character of this potential employee revitalize our working conditions?
>
> Can the creative character of this potential employee crank up the environment of collaboration?
>
> Can the creative character of this potential employee help lead others in attaining high performance goals?
>
> Can the creative character of this potential employee improve our ability to approach matters creatively?

If you can address just a little bit of some of these concerns in your presentation, making a good impression in the process, you have succeeded in moving toward a personal, face-to-face meeting, at which point you can throw the bioblog into the trash can because you no longer need it. It's just a tool, and a disposable one at that.

2

OUT WITH THE OLD, IN WITH THE NEW

THE GOAL OF A BIOBLOG IS TO GET YOU AN INTERVIEW. They have no limits and they have no more boundaries than a typical web page on the Internet. There are no rules, other than good taste and what makes sense. *Whatever gets the job done is okay.* Essentially, whether they're ink on paper or shot across webspace electronically, bioblogs are the first cousins to web pages, part and parcel to the World Wide Web of work. Integrating two powerful elements—snappy graphics and enticing text—they are a new form of self-marketing, advertising your competitive potential through snazzy presentations as demanding as pop-ups, but much more curious, personal, and informing: in other words, value added.

As an emerging art form that borrows generously from the techniques of traditional collage, professional photography, painting, and typography, it is a natural medium for those creative souls who desire to express more of their inner, deeper selves than has been possible in the standard operating formats of "chronological" or "functional" résumés. These new visual feasts chronicle one's ability to make a statement, and their sole function and singular purpose is to establish serious, first contact with the strongest first impression.

They are not another version of e-résumés, as modern e-résumés have done little more than drag the drab and mundane formats of typical printed résumés into the pixelated, scroll-and-click environment of web portfolios and blogs, adding color and pizzazz but still lacking the necessary, deeper shades of a candidate's real creative character and personality. Cluttering up an already overwrought résumé with stock art images does nothing to make it special.

To this day, the gazillions of résumés floating around "out there" and the ones presented in the sample sections of typical résumé books are almost completely dedicated to a person's *past:* all the accomplishments, work history, experience, skills, training, and education applied and used elsewhere, sometime ago (some recently, but most of it not so recent), for somebody else for some other purposes and in some different conditions, all in past tense; yet most "average" work seekers would be happy to have one of these cleaned-up, polished-up résumés, especially if it was rendered for them into an acceptable e-form in a painless manner.

However, there are some glaring, problematic shortcomings with these outdated, shabby-underneath-their-shiny-surface résumés that profess to get their points across so well:

- They look too similar because their plans are the same, and form follows plans.
- They tend to reveal way too much of the person's impersonal "story."
- What's missing is often more important than what's included.
- Revealing extraneous details blurs the picture of the person behind them.
- People forget (or don't know) how people "look the same" on their résumés.
- People don't understand how tired or lazy people are "on the other end."

Résumés are not affidavits or business cards; they are the bait in the river as the job-hoppers try to lure in a big catch. As even beginner fishermen and -women know, using the wrong bait makes the whole endeavor pointless.

HIDDEN MESSAGE

What is generally missing even in the best of buttoned and menued e-résumés is a tangible sense of the person's creative character traits. Typically the traits are implied in a loose string of adjectives attached to overall qualifications, such as "dedicated to the unfettered freedom of artistic expression," "a savvy businessperson with the vision and drive to overcome obstacles and excel in a competitive marketplace," "proven ability to lead by example and inspire loyalty," "ability to motivate staff," and "goal-driven."

Occasionally, the format and graphics stuck onto the e-résumé pages give us a hint that the person is creative, but barely a glimpse is revealed of how that might be applied to a greater range of criteria, such as in sales, marketing, management, or some other business arena. They're weak in structure and not enticing enough for us really to want to know more about the person. Inasmuch as they may be a notch or two more curious and interesting than the endless stream of "same-old" résumés that batter the e-mail boxes and posting sites of the electronic work world, they still fall short of standing up and shouting, "Look at me!" They still get lost in the chum that is thrown overboard to attract the sharks.

As appropriate as word strings and iconic images may be to imply or symbolize personal strengths, they do little to paint a picture of the person as a whole human being with a developed and unique character. A black-and-white photograph would make up for this insufficiency because we can read an immeasurable amount of information in a face. Most people usually don't want to post a photo so anonymously, so there must be an alternative to resolve the problem of "flattened résumés."

How can we generate a sense of "the wholeness" of the individual who lingers in wait behind the simple words and phrases that describe him or her—the actual living person who is eventually going to be hired? What *exactly is it* that we need to offer something new and different? I'll tell you what: bioblogs. And bioblogs are not for everybody, which is why they have the power of potential. They will be the new wave, and you can be on the crest of it if you want to put in the hard work and determined effort.

INVENTORIES

I started writing résumés in 1971 as a young apprentice to an old pro writer on Fifth Avenue and Forty-second Street, the heart of midtown Manhattan, and, at the time, the heat core of capitalism for the free world. Ann H. Tanners, who had started America's first professional résumé writing service in 1942, taught me everything she knew, along with Robert A. S. Sullivan, who was the Latin American sales rep for the U.S. Chamber of Commerce. My five years under their truculent wings were worth a golden Ph.D. at Harvard as far as writing for print goes, and during my tenure I wrote the life stories of such people as the NYPD chief of detectives who was forced out during the Serpico scandal, the marketing director who made Gatorade® a household name, a famous opera star, a few hotshot diplomats, and thousands of regular workplace people in virtually every occupation. I learned a lot about creative character and what it means in the American workplace.

In those pioneering days, "job résumés" were used almost exclusively by senior level executives and managers (mostly men) who were VIPs in the topmost tiers of their companies. They ruled, and they were exceedingly demanding with regard to how their careers were written about. (Often confidentially.) Way back then, résumés were termed "personal inventories," and traditional formats were religiously chronological and included under the category of "personal data" such items as "no debt encumbrances" and "Christian worker," as well as names of their wives and children (and their ages), what church they went to, and their "hobbies and interests" (generally geared to what they thought prospective employers would think looked good, such as golf, tennis, sailing, or baseball). That was then—the Modern Stone Age; and this is now—the Slippery Slope of the Knowledge Age.

By the mid-1960s résumés were increasingly used as job-search tools by mid-level management workers lower down in the organizational ranks as well, but primarily by people who were still employed—i.e., by people who were looking for another or better job, rather than people who were out of work. If someone back then said he was "working on his résumé" it wasn't immediately assumed by his peers that he had been fired or downsized, but that he was ready to make a move up the ladder somewhere.

By the mid-1970s the "personal inventory" handle fell by the wayside, sometimes traded for the confidential, anonymous tag of "John Smith (Pseudonym)" and with the current employer carefully disguised, as in "a large supplier of wholesale paper goods" or "a retail operation in fifteen southern states." (I occasionally had clients show up from the same company who inadvertently crossed each other's path at the elevator, which they considered bad luck; I soon learned to schedule appointments so this wouldn't happen.)

A typical résumé had to be at least two and preferably three or four pages long to be considered sufficiently substantial; anything less seemed too unimportant by the people who used them on their way up the corporate ladder. They were almost always printed on parchment paper, which had a more expensive feel and gave them an added psychological "worthiness" value. My clients were quite selective about to whom they sent them, and usually went to the trouble to type a "cover letter" for their résumés. Bolder and braver clients employed a shotgun approach, mailing out résumés to a couple of hundred companies at a time, which was then seen as an expensive, broad marketing strategy. (It wouldn't impress anyone now.)

I will never forget how much I had to battle my mentors to convince them that it was time to start changing résumés to one-pagers. They argued that it was bad for our business, since most of the labor-intensive work was in the initial interview—getting the missing data down on paper—and in the writing/rewriting (to the customer's satisfaction) of the first page, which had not only the "executive summary" but also the bulk of the most recent job and difficult-to-render experience. I countered: That's my point. Why bother with additional pages? Charge more for one, and focus on the most recent job!

In most résumés, what followed the first page's most important information was less-revealing chronological history: previous employment, education, etc. That's where we made our money, charging for the pages that took nothing more than a little bit of typing; they were fluffed out and white spaced. I had to convince my bosses that one-page résumés were what the market needed, that we could charge more for their "special service." If we could get more money for less writing time, less printing labor, and less ink and paper, why not? They resisted, but the plan finally proved itself.

TELEGRAPHING

Eventually, I wrote my first book, *The Résumé Writer's Handbook*. At that time, 1978, there was only one other résumé book on the shelves, Arco's two-decade-old *Résumés That Get Jobs*. I introduced new and succinct one-page formats, and offered how-to guides, such as the "Key Telegraphic Terminology," which is found in various forms in most career and résumé books.

Since then, a whole lot of things have changed, the biggest one being the advent of the Internet and the creation of such commercial enterprises as monster. com, hotjobs.com, and tens of thousands of other work-, career-, and candidate-related websites and businesses that provide an extraordinarily broad range of services—from résumé and letter development to career counseling and recruiting. Now there are seemingly limitless résumé books filling the shelves.

In 1983, I got out of the business. I was burned out from interviewing every day ten or more people who were caught up in hostile takeovers, and I was weary from having to listen to all their problems, complaints, mistakes, failed promises, and personal sorrows. Other than writing a second edition of my book in 1986, until 2003, I paid not the slightest attention to the world of résumé writing. The only résumé I wrote was my own, which was hard enough to keep up with.

Then, in 2004, I started combing résumé/career books to see what the experts had to say. I was curious what the Internet had wreaked on them. What I found stunned me. The authors tended to regurgitate the same information about how to write and distribute a résumé. It's not that the information was not good advice, because it was—and still is (for what it's worth)—but it was and still is standard operating procedure, which even the authors occasionally admitted doesn't guarantee anything in terms of competing with the huge numbers of résumés in orbit each and every day. (An estimated twenty million plus circulating the web, according to monster.com, who ought to know!)

Other than Richard Nelson Bolles's *What Color Is Your Parachute?*, most of these books are show-and-tell guides for reticent writers to learn how to turn a lousy résumé into a better one, or, if you work really hard at it, to make yours as good as the rest of the millions out there. There's a lot of relevant information about job hunting as well, but as far as the personalizing aesthetics of résumés is concerned, they're pretty much dead ends in terms of originality. It makes sense, because they can't make you do it, and you are the one who has to figure out how to do it.

That's it. That's as far as they go. They stop short of the finish line. They don't take you into the next realm, the important one: how to make your résumé reflect the true you.

E-résumés don't fare any better. They are as ethereal, poofy, fuzzy, and disjointed as all other e-things whipped around by the flapping, directionless, howling winds of the Internet, that *Great Emptiness Encompassing Everything! (GEEE!)*. Personally, for me, what's worse is that there're so many résumés out there that they seem to have lost their aggregate heft and any significant weightiness, or what they call gravitas in politics.

TO THE FUTURE

Now that we've arrived headfirst into the twenty-first century, and are inextricably committed to doing things differently (*meaning,* we *have* to), it is time for résumés to take a quantum leap into their next natural phase. The résumé calls out for a Picasso to save it from sameness, and I, as an artist and writer, have taken on the challenge.

Now, if I had the ability to redirect the ebb and flow of business trends, I would take today's résumés straight into what I call *nanoblogs,* miniature holographs of our applicant selves that could be "turned on" (animated) in a "virtualizing arena" (a fully dimensional platform) in a stranger's private environment, so that rather than looking at our record—a log that recounts the work history of what we did rather than who we are—the prospective "money offerer" would be able to see us "money seekers" as "engaged in person"—making our sales pitch, our little nano-doppelgängers selling our potential right there on their spot, in their airspace, talking straight to, and at, them. Eventually, in OS version 303.1188.191, they might be people-skills programmed to "soft talk with them," responding to their questions for us, preloaded for bear, as it were. (Now *that* would take *confidence of character!*)

Matter of fact, I am going on record right here and now that this event will eventually happen. I'd put money on it. It's surely down the line, and probably less than twenty years away, no more a technological leap than Dick Tracy's nifty watch a millennium ago.

In the interim, until nano- and genetic-technologies catch up with this handy utilitarian concept, we will have to settle for today's bioblogs, graphically enhanced résumés that can be both printed and sent electronically, which will provide someone "out there" on the employing side of the table with an improved, enlightened, and embellished sense of our true creative characteristics.

Why is that so important? Because who we are is the most important thing in this business of them and us, companies and employees, hirers and new hires.

Hiring already is and will continue in the foreseeable future to be more about who you will become than who you have been. It isn't a process focused on your bank of knowledge and hard skills, but it's aimed at how well you can work with the subtle, emotionally tactile people-expressed dynamics of your managers and coworkers. Factual data associated with your roles and interactions in group teamwork can (and will) be obtained, scrutinized, and compared, but for the purposes of hiring a real-life person, the ultimate calculus is going to be in your creative character and how well you present it.

What a prospective employer wants to know is, What kind of character are you, and will you be someone who is good for us to have on our team? What kind of player will you turn out to be? How well can we predict your future, from what you offer? Are you who you claim you are? Who are you going to be when you succeed or fail, get yourself cornered by a major problem, slapped about by the nearest competitor, or dressed down by a disgruntled customer? How will you react when faced with these difficult situations?

These are the big questions; answer them well and you will be on your way. It doesn't have to get any more complicated than that. Creative character is what employers are paying for, not just skills, which are a given and presumed to be readily available, in finished form: you either have them in the state the employers need or you don't. That's the easy part, because it's only a small part of what employers look for when they hire.

Creative character is what employers are looking for, and it's what's needed on résumés today and tomorrow. It's also what has been blatantly missing in action, although it hasn't been as much of a problem until recently. But with today's astronomical numbers being zipped and zapped back and forth in the expanding and contracting universe of Work—and the mysterious, alchemical admixtures of our fiercely competitive talent pool—it is now apparent that creative characters must come out of their politically and culturally safe closets.

No one will notice if we keep hiding.

The time for cowering and crossing fingers is long gone.

The old order is over.

One thing the Internet has accomplished is to render accountability naked and immediate: you not only are what you are, you can't escape it even for a minute.

USING BIOBLOGS

How do you make a powerful first impression when it counts? Just like people do on countless web pages, by combining striking graphics (loaded with subliminal clues) with super writing (rendered in psychological typography). With bioblogs, the information *is there,* but it's loaded to the hilt, oozing with connotations that are interwoven with the rest of the elements for a "strength of multitude" impact. Rather than relying totally on "I did this and that," the new bioblogs flash subliminal information while emphasizing "I am this" and "I can do that," and, more important, "I am different."

That's what the résumé business, as baiting, is all about, isn't it? Being different. For if you were satisfied with being the same, why bother? That's plain enough. To a prospective employer, a person's employable past is increasingly irrelevant as a reason to hire someone, which in turn renders the candidate's future increasingly important as an element in the screening process. This progression is completely logical, and it's a development that was inevitable. We are where we are now because résumés have simply faltered over time like tires worn down by the road—they're just about at the end of their usefulness. Employers have about as much luck figuring out who someone "is" from an average résumé as they would probing over a flat tire and examining the wear pattern to figure out what kind of person has been driving the car. That's why you need a bioblog to show what you can do.

ART FORM

Résumés as templates are over. Click art is as passé as the mummies stacked up in Egyptian tombs. As I say, *bioblogs are a brand-new art form.* They're not for everyone. They're for you only if you are so creative and resourceful that you are driven and self-motivated to put yourself above the average Joe and Mary of the regular résumé crowd.

Every creative person who desires to perform at a maximum level has within him a unique potentiality for a critical resourcefulness, which can be brought to bear in a thousand different ways through his array of individual traits: inspiring confidence, engendering trust, probing new solutions, pursuing objectives tenaciously, adding optimism to the team, speaking out for integrity, imposing order on chaos, exploring new concepts, and in many other ways.

Because we workers share an inverted atmosphere, an upside-down world where shortsighted managers and outmoded policies force similar workers into the same boxes, as strong creative individuals we must promote our potential rather than the skimpy facts of limiting experiences. As job seekers or job holders, we are in a bit of a fix. Traditional workplace prejudices place an unrealistic importance on the credentials *of the former*: education and experience. The smartest move we can make is to present the best face of our creative character, and show the resourcefulness it stands for, despite how the routine of our workplace conditions may have stifled our innovative attempts and successes.

For you candidates who long to perform at your highest level, you may have suffered an ordeal of career moves that continually thwarted your efforts to contribute, that dampened your enthusiasm, and that often undercut your loyalty to a company's well-being. It may likely be a pattern that overshadows your future career steps with much apprehension.

I'm happy to report that times are changing, and hope is inching its way across the electronic farmlands and up the walls of techno-scrapers from the Third Coast to the Nanobelt, where today global business success means survival of the organizationally fittest—those who perform well as individual entities on a world stage, and who rely greatly on their creative capital rather than on shelf-bought technology. In an emerging service-oriented economy spread across the far-flung marketplace, the value of human ingenuity (already the prime factor in the equation) has become the issue.

So how can we get more *creative?*

The answer is *bioblogs*.

GREAT CHARACTER COMBOS
FROM THE
AMERICAN WORKPLACE MENU

RESOURCEFUL & CHEERFUL & TENACIOUS
WORK STYLE

**Looks for hidden solutions to problems with a good
attitude and much notable effort.**

COMPETITIVE & CONVINCING & OUTSPOKEN
WORK STYLE

**Spearheads targeting by nurturing strong leadership and
providing an unquestioned commitment.**

ASSERTIVE & CONSIDERATE & VIGOROUS
WORK STYLE

**Clear leadership with enhanced openness
that energizes communication and spirit.**

INSPIRING & INNOVATIVE & INTEGRATING
WORK STYLE

**Self-assurance packaged with adept skills that easily
and successfully involve others fully.**

CONFIDENT & PATIENT & EVEN-TEMPERED
WORK STYLE

**Possesses a framework that encompasses
an orderly and direct approach to goals.**

OPTIMISTIC & COOPERATIVE & ACCOMMODATING

Work Style

**Resourceful at bringing the most out of team members'
creative characters and motivating them.**

OPEN-MINDED & EMPATHETIC & RECEPTIVE

Work Style

**Gains support through a genuine concern for others through
keen, reliable, and constant listening skills.**

PRACTICAL & INDUSTRIOUS & OBLIGING

Work Style

**Headstrong and gets things done with a no-nonsense approach;
appreciates teamwork but can forge on without it.**

SELF-RELIANT & ANIMATED & LOYAL

Work Style

**Looks ahead rather than at the past; brings a sense of
momentum and clear purpose to the mission.**

PERSISTENT & POSITIVE & CAUTIOUS

Work Style

**Thinks matters through while analyzing risks versus rewards;
is not distracted by negative details.**

AGREEABLE & GENEROUS & GENTLE

Work Style

**Sympathetic to coworkers' needs; a facilitator
who smooths ruffled feathers with expertise.**

CONSTRUCTIVE & RELIABLE & INSTRUCTIVE

WORK STYLE

An idea generator through thick and thin; avoids future crises
by teaching others how to handle problems.

GROUNDED & IMPARTIAL & ETHICAL

WORK STYLE

Respected for sharing a sense of integrity; evenly
principled, with sound foundation in what's fair and sensible.

ENTERPRISING & DETERMINED & SELF-DISCIPLINED

WORK STYLE

Innovative and entrepreneurial; self-driven and and
self-managed, yet is open to ideas even if not proven.

PERSUASIVE & ENERGIZED & TACTFUL

WORK STYLE

A natural seller who employs good sense and understanding to
energize communication to keep aiming at a target.

PRINCIPLED & ASSIDUOUS & HONORABLE

WORK STYLE

An old-school type who is what he or she says, the pillar of
a company's reputation and willing to stake everything on it.

CONSISTENT & VITAL & TRUSTWORTHY

WORK STYLE

A leader at any level due to values and constructive strengths
of predictability, which carries weight with skeptical workers.

CIRCUMSPECT & SELF-AWARE & POISED

Work Style

Disciplined examiner of self who looks within to see signs of the larger picture, and to others for necessary ingredients.

PRAGMATIC & LOYAL & DIPLOMATIC

Work Style

Sees hard facts and human data as equal weights to measure on scale of truth: not concerned about looks or attitudes.

FORTHRIGHT & BALANCED & JUST

Work Style

Frank by nature but not overbearing; an inclusive negotiator of conflicting views especially when differences conflict.

GOOD-NATURED & BOLD & CONTROLLED

Work Style

An audacious leader with a strong attitude; can handle big fears and failures and let the chips fall in tough times.

3

CREATING A BIOBLOG

BIOBLOGS COMBINE COMMON SENSE AND CREATIVITY. They join to produce the most visually exciting and interesting bios we can design. They are about the future you, not the half-emptied-shell-of-your-past you; they crystallize the creative you of now. There're only a few things you need to remember.

PRINCIPLE NO. 1

They're only bait.

In other words, be ready to cut the line.

However, there's bait—and then there's Bait. Good bait. Better bait. Best bait. Like pornography and beauty, you'll know it when you see it. You won't have any doubt that you're looking at it if your creative juices are still flowing through your pipes.

PRINCIPLE NO. 2

Always use the best bait.

In other words, switch bait for different fish.

Since the 1940s when the first résumés were designed by Ann Tanners in her paper-cluttered office, the sole purpose they have ever "been for" is to be used as a lure to get a prospective employer hooked on you and your package of personality, skills, experience, and knowledge. In a nutshell, they're just bait.

PRINCIPLE NO. 3

Don't tell the whole story.

In other words, don't try to land the fish in the boat until you have a good bite.

Timing is everything, in fishing and careering. Tease them; make them hungry for more; be ready to deliver it at the right moment; and then reel them in. Make them wonder what else you have to offer. After all, what's the point of putting everything out front, especially since words rarely depict *the real you of your true creative character* accurately enough to give someone a good idea of who you really are? Providing more mundane information is not the key to improving the corporate bait.

Today, we are dealing with a new set of problems—the sheer number of résumés competing for attention and the best jobs, the incredibly demanding criteria of discriminating employers for whom we desire to work, and the continuing emphasis on creative resourcefulness rather than impressive lists of previous achievements.

Let us not be numbed or shaken by these new challenges; rather, let's take on a proactive strategy to turn them into an opportunity to showcase our intuitive character traits, to show how we as individuals are truly different from the rest of the pack. Let's not be afraid to stand out and speak, and speak with no apologies for being an expressive individual, showing right up front what we believe and how we think, what we know and are able to admit, and what we have learned from our experiences.

We do not have to hide inside the guise of so-called "objective résumés" any longer. Bioblogs are just a natural creative intrusion into the worn-out world of résumés, where everybody beats everybody else to the punch with their long lists.

RULES OF THE ROAD

Just as I established some of the first rules of résumés in *The Résumé Writer's Handbook* and its two editions over twenty-three years, I offer a few guiding principles for future *Bioblogs*. They will help you determine if you have created a good combination of images and text for the marketplace of talent in which you choose to compete.

YOUR BIOBLOG

Should
1. Convey a sense of your creative character through an exciting visual style.
2. Be creative enough to be informing and interesting.

3. Inspire curiosity by highlighting important information.
4. Paint a picture of your personality with the fewest words.
5. Sketch your work style through an encompassing form.
6. Seem global in scope although it will be used locally.

Should not
1. Appear cluttered and uncertain in focus or direction.
2. Be hard to relate to when applied to specific places.
3. Inspire ridicule by pretending to be more than you are.
4. Communicate without tangible strength of personal vitality.
5. Be limited to the narrow target of a single title.
6. Try to be a letter and résumé and application form simultaneously.

Obviously, common sense must prevail no matter what other factors are taken into account. I don't recommend your putting a photo of yourself spread out like Odalisque on Freud's couch, or posting a mug shot of yourself in a hair shirt, but you could spotlight yourself atop a rock canyon you've just climbed, standing before a technical library in which you spent a decade studying, or surrounded by children with whom you have worked closely to nurture and of whom are tremendously, personally proud. If there's an important emotional connection with true meaning to your character, I say use it. People can stand up as individuals only with feelings, thoughts, and ideas resulting from their experience, not neutered and diminished as numbers.

The most significant difference from the old days is that *it's all about you,* this new form, and there's no need to hide the "I," as was done for decades in traditional résumés. The "I" can come out of the closet now, well rested and ready for action, thank you very much. The "I" can stand up and shout: "I'm back. I know who I am. I know what I want. I know where I'm going. I know what I can do for you. I know what I can become if you give me the opportunity and tools to show you."

There are two essential elements to any creative bioblog regardless of the particular single, framed-page visual form it takes:

• Graphics and Visualization
  This establishes the psychological mood of your statement and is a subtle expression of your character: bold, contemplative, playful, witty, determined, resourceful . . . a silent silhouette of your inner self, sort of the first impression of your "public face."

- Syntax and Context
  This is your data message expressed through grammar (words) and controlled through judicious typography (form). It complements your visualized image by voicing a parallel statement of you and your originality.

The combinations of these elements can be elementary or complex; the mutually supporting relationship between words overlaying pictures/images and their underlying context brings a completely new quality to your message as a result of *the strength of magnitude*: i.e., the power of the visual imagery inextricably woven with the information in words combines to make an impact much stronger than either would have separately. It is the effect of deconstruction.

In this new form, anything goes, as long as it works; they are not for the average Joe Blow, who would be happy just to have a sensible, well-typed résumé that reports the bland facts of his experience and education. Bioblogs are handmade by and for the most creative people in the talent pool, like you, the ones over whom the best employers are beating their heads against the wall, trying to find a way to reach out and establish a relationship while you are still happily employed somewhere else. (Take a look at William Poundstone's *How Would You Move Mount Fuji* to peek into this lofty world of best hires.)

Any image you choose can accompany text formatted in any scheme or design you prefer, from contrasting images to images that are quietly resident in the background, providing a mood or undertone for your statement. Just as on any web page, there are endless possibilities of approaches to presenting your particular character traits and individual preferences. It's up to you to decide to what degree you want to impress a company with your creative abilities and resourcefulness. You can take a serious approach, a humorous one, or one that rings true from media exposure—playing against a popular ad campaign, for example—as long as you don't turn it into a cliché.

Your bioblog, being a snapshot of your creativity, innovation, and resourcefulness, must not fall into the trap of being too clever by half; it must maintain a sense of integrity and class. First drafts probably won't be smooth or subtle enough.

Again, it's all up to you, but your main task is to make the strongest first impression that you can. According to Malcolm Gladwell in *Blink: The Power of Thinking Without Thinking,* these first impressions tend to occur in less than two seconds, which is why the subliminal visual imagery is so critical: employers get it subconsciously before they even read the words, so the graphic content is more like the first bait, and the words are the wiggle, the tease.

What you want to accomplish through your instant message of self-confidence and self-assurance (because that's one of the many things employers want) is that *you know who you are, what you want, why you're reaching out to them, what you know, and what you can do.* Remember that how you use the bioblog will suffice to provide some of the aforementioned points.

From these slices-of-your-character ingredients, stirred up in the pot of your self-promotion—the picture of your interior persona that bioblogs allow—you can make a statement about your potential without hammering some stranger with all the dull stuff you do or have done, which really don't make a lot of sense without being able to provide (in person) the parameters of the actual conditions in which you did (or didn't, or couldn't) do them. There is so much to your story that it doesn't make much sense to tell just a little bit of it.

The bioblog is designed to generate an interview, at which you'll have the opportunity to express yourself openly and intelligently and to fill in the workplace details that cannot possibly be presented or adequately explained in any résumé. This has always been one of my main objections to relying on résumés to communicate "what happened," since workplace dynamics and interworker psychologies are so complicated, as well as the demeanor of the bosses, that little makes sense until the situations can be described more fully. Minor achievements can really be quite noteworthy in some circumstance, while major accomplishments may not be such a big deal in light of other facts. In the world of work, things are generally more complicated than they seem at first glance.

From my experience, which covers manufacturing, health care, sales, marketing, publishing, construction, and a half-dozen other fields, and from interviewing some five thousand résumé clients as well as hundreds of corporate workers (when rewriting job descriptions and performance evaluations), I believe most résumés are truly illusory with regard to *telling the story.* They leave out not only the primary facets of the "owner's" creative character traits, but they ignore the working character traits of bosses and peers, conditions that largely determine how successful a person can be at her job. (If you don't believe me, ask someone who worked at Enron, Arthur Andersen, WorldCom, AIG, HealthSouth, Kmart, Tyco, or Morgan Stanley.)

An additional benefit of bioblogs is to offset this omission by focusing so intensely on the personal creative character of the candidate, hopefully sparking curiosity and interest so you will be called to come into an employer's office and tell the "rest of the story." They certainly know that the résumé won't tell the real or whole story, so why continue to pretend by rigging up e-résumés and web portfolios with bar charts and graphs of sales performance, or details about field responsibilities and operations management functions, which ultimately seem dull and hackneyed.

Why not slap them in the face like Socrates did to his students when they "got" his point?

Here! See this? This is me! I'm different! Get it?

DISPATCHES

At the end of the bioblog work tunnel is a way station, and on the lonely platform stands a solitary man or woman, *a tribal receiver,* who will take your primitive message and feed it into a supercomputing rack of interviewers' servers. These servers will then dissect and digest with their neural-electron laser-beamed microscopes every claim and point stop in your bioblog. If successful, yours will throw a wrench into the internal guts of the machine and make it spit yours out: just be ready for an alien-level intrusion into your personal creative self by the automatons that monitor the meters and gauges.

God knows exactly what they're looking for—you probably won't be able to decipher it. All you can do is be who you are, and who you are becoming, and hope for serendipity, coincidence, good timing, or guardian angels to make all the dots connect or the planets line up. But that's the nature of the beast, *finding good work,* and that's never going to change completely. Just as sled draggers in King Tut's time ran out of pyramids to work on and had to move into new high-tech jobs (hieroglyphic pop-up ads, perhaps), so will we, our children, and theirs: it's the nature of work and the free economies in which work prevails.

There will never be a format for any kind of document that will eliminate all of the unknowns, so the best thing to do is to keep betting on the horse we have the most reliable stats on—*our selves*—and what we know and believe our creative character can do in the last stretch of the race, where the American "can-do" quality really counts.

Our ploy, of course, is to catch the workplace umpires and screening referees off guard, while they're not looking. We want to take advantage of every opportunity to make our mark well before we are laid out like J. Alfred Prufrock's specimens on a table. We need to disarm them before they think to blink, by enticing them to "engage with us" while they are looking at (registering and assimilating) our bioblogs. We need to help them get their minds off "the stuff of us" and see more of "us as we are." They're human beings who have jobs, too, aren't they, these corporate gatekeepers, so this should not be an impossible mission, right?

We just need to help them, which is why they are easy prey for the powerful *whoomp!* of a beautiful bioblog, as you shall see in the gallery in Chapter 4.

BARRIERS BROKEN

What you don't have to do in bioblogs is list every job and every company and every academic program that you have accumulated. That's the old way. You don't have to aim everything at a company's job title either, because your talents and creative character are a composite. The ruling principle is to match your creativity with the creative level and style of the corporate culture you are trying to join. That's the only match about which you need to worry. Customize according to conditions. You will find that the more time you work on creating a striking bioblog, the more ideas you will come up with for additional versions. As you move through the world around you, surrounded by flashing graphics and shouting content (particularly advertising), you will begin to see ways to borrow and alter some of those images for your own use, and it is completely acceptable to use contemporary ad campaign strategies in your own workplace strategies, especially if they are clever and noteworthy. However, be careful to avoid turning your campaign into a cliché or letting your message become amateurish, silly, or ill conceived. Keep your act classy, no matter what. If you are in doubt about something, don't include it.

You'll notice these bioblogs are not a litany of chronologies, duties, and accomplishments. This is a blind date that takes some tact, a slow dance before getting down and boogeying.

GLOBAL GALLERY

The following gallery is to show you what bioblogs look like. They are presented for the sake of stimulating your creativity, so you can see the many ways to bring your own personal attributes and experiences into these new frameworks. Whether they end up as ink on paper or as a jpeg file in your web portfolio or blog site, they are designed to put your best foot forward and not to tell the whole story.

My solutions to technical problems are usually as simple as I can get away with. With regard to distributing a bioblog after you create it (or pay someone else to do it for you), print it in black-and-white (or color), scan it, save it as a jpeg, tiff, pdf, or any other format you may desire, compress it if you need to, and then have it ready as an image file that can simply be opened and viewed easily by your targeted person or company.

If you want to get really fancy, you could convert it into a pdf, which is the ideal format that just about anyone can open on a desktop computer. It's up to you how much technology you want to plug into it. Post it in your blog, e-mail it as an attachment, or mail or fax it. I would not suggest trying to convert it into an electronic e-résumé with buttons and menus because it's too much work and would break the rule of not saying too much. Do a completely different résumé for that purpose if you need to because the e-résumé building process is unwieldy and can be difficult, even for those who are well versed in it.

Take advantage of the web portfolio–posting technology and let employers and worker-seekers come to you, especially if you are currently employed and therefore highly chased after. (A recent *Wall Street Journal* article pointed out how much more desirable candidates are who are on the job, and how firms are trying to comb the marketplace to reach out to them.) Make them come to you, and have the "right stuff" ready when they find you.

From the following samples you could cut and paste, borrow from or trade out parts, to meet your particular needs. Think of some theme that is relevant to who you are, your true inner character, and make it shout—but subtly. I think you will find that building a bioblog can be a lot of fun.

FYI: these were all created in QuarkXPress 6.1, with images scanned and Photoshopped, but you can use whatever software works best for you and your computer fluency.

Good luck creating your . . . best bait.

P.S.: If you wonder if these are "real," I would say they are as close to being real (based on truth, that is) as most other résumés, which, in my estimation—from my vast experience and firsthand knowledge—are generally about 70 percent "true" and 20 percent "distorted," with the remaining 10 percent an unknown, attributed to "bad memory" and "benefit of the doubt." If anything is relative in the world of résumés/bioblogs, it's "the truth." (Your truth may be a different version from your peers, which could well be different from your boss's.)

This is why my approach to a powerful visual and textual merging opens the door for the details to be provided later, because that's when the truth really counts—and when it should be brought to the table. Your best bet is to provide the big picture, which is more accurate than the little paddings of a résumé, which can be assumed, and are therefore somewhat shallow.

Don't get sidetracked: stick to the important matters of who you are, what you offer, what kind of creative thinker you are. Show them from the first impression. If you wait, it may be too late.

KEY QUESTIONS

Bioblogs need to touch upon the shades of gray that lie in the shadows of the expansive array of questions employers are prepared to ask a prospective employee. It would be impossible for a résumé of any type to deal with all of these myriad issues without turning into a lengthy essay or a book. Thus, I offer the following short list of the most pertinent questions posed to a job seeker in the normal questioning of a skilled interrogator.

There are six main categories of queries that relate to you and either your past experience, present qualifications, or future plans and overall potential. Any question will be specifically relevant to your self-promotion and your *I am, I want, I can, I know, I will,* and ***We'll just have to see how it turns out.***

These questions should always be mentally familiar as you prepare your words and graphics, for they will be in your future if you are successful—maybe not all of them, but certainly some of them, and perhaps a lot of them. It's like preparing for the SATs: you cannot practice too much, as you will affirm when you sit down with a pencil and the clock starts ticking.

Rehearse and practice. Pick someone with whom to partner and run through your answers until you are comfortable with them and they make sense to you. Think about how your bioblog can lead you into a discussion of your creative character traits that will reflect well on you while still allowing you to remain honest and open to further questioning.

Think about how your bioblog can address these looming and underlying issues that are on the mind of an employer.

MOST RELEVANT QUESTIONS

Your Creative Character's "I Am"

- **What are some of the most creative things you have done?**
- **What are the most important characteristics you are looking for in a job? Why?**
- **What qualities are important to determine whom you would hire for this job?**
- **How do you think our company determines someone's success?**
- **What is the most intellectually challenging thing you're looking for at work?**

- Why do you think you would like it and could handle it?
- What is the most intellectually challenging thing you've done?
- How did you determine your career choice?
- What's most valuable to you: high pay, or job recognition and advancement?
- What would a ladder of success look like organizationally to you? Why?
- If you could construct your own job with us, what factors would you include?

Your Creative Character's "I Want"
- Why do you feel you can be successful in this position?
- What is your greatest strength?
- What is your greatest weakness?
- What is the chain that links your strength and weaknesses?
- How do you respond to being put on the spot?
- What's going on at your present job that disturbs you?

Your Creative Character's "I Can"
- What is your most significant accomplishment? Why?
- Under what conditions have you been most successful in a difficult undertaking?
- How hard do you work to achieve your objectives?
- Has your competition had an impact on your achieving goals? How?
- What will be your earning potential five years from now?

Your Creative Character's "I Know"
- In what ways have you demonstrated maturity by leading?
- What has satisfied you most in your employment experiences?
- What factors determine your personal choices in life?
- Should others do the same as you?
- What would you do differently?
- How did you respond to your greatest disappointment?
- What are the most important rewards you expect from your job?
- Under what circumstances have your associates relied upon you?
- In your terms, what is a professional?

Your Creative Character's "I Will"
- How do you influence someone to accept your ideas?
- How good are you at presentations?
- How are your verbal skills compared to your writing skills?
- How should supervisors and subordinates interact in the workplace?
- How would you be described by a close friend?
- How do you get along with coworkers?

The Tricky Part

There's also some confidence-jolting questions employers like to throw onto the poker table to keep you on your toes, like asking how you would move Mount Fiji: they want to see how you think and to determine what you would do under intellectual pressure. This is an ideal opportunity to prime your wit pump and get incisive, as well as to show them how much you are up-to-date on current events and business/technology trends. This is also when you can introduce some of your personal interests or defuse some old baggage without sidestepping a significant issue.

YOUR CREATIVE CHARACTER & WILD CARDS

Spontaneous Response Queries
- How did you prepare for this interview?
- What are your short-term and long-term personal goals?
- How would you create a plan for your team if you were in charge?
- How important are details?
- What types of situations get you down?
- What do you do when you know you're right, but others disagree with you?
- Do you feel qualified to be successful in your position? Why?
- If not, what will you do to compensate for your deficiencies?
- Fill in the blank: "Successful managers should _____."
- Fill in the blank: "Teammates working well together should _____."
- How well do you work under pressure?

The Playful Part

When they come around the bend and start to like what they see and want to try one more time to call your bluff, be prepared for this sort of encounter:

How creative are you?

Can you still haul the wood?

What makes you think so?

Can we believe you?

And Finally

Can you come in and let us have a look at you?

CHAPTER 4

THE BIOBLOG GALLERY

THE 100 BIOBLOGS SHOWN IN THE FOLLOWING GALLERY COVER A BROAD RANGE OF INDIVIDUALS' PARTICULAR STRATEGIES AND PLANS FOR FINDING CHALLENGING WORK, BUT THEY ALL SHARE A COMMON QUALITY—CREATIVE DRIVE. These examples of "creative breakthrough bioblogs" are presented in order that you may see the many ways you can create your own unique presentation of your creative skills—and the best bait for your purposes.

ORGANIZATION NOTES

Since these bioblogs are not arranged in any particular order, such as alphabetically by name or "objective" or field of endeavor, I have simply assigned them numbers and indicated their name and major graphic concept so you can bookmark those you may want to use for your own template. I hope this will help you keep track of them.

Chapter 5, "How to Build a Bioblog," will walk you through the process of creating a bioblog from scratch. (I offer two examples of the process, for a man and a woman.) You will notice that these are all black-and-white graphic images, which I believe are sufficiently powerful without wandering into the overwhelming complexities of digitized color, which will be technically more challenging in terms of producing and transferring to others as computer files.

LIST OF ONE HUNDRED BIOBLOGS

No.	NAME	KEY GRAPHIC THEME	FIELD OF WORK OR EXPERTISE
1	Joseph Ballatino	Manly Strength	Commercial Construction Management
2	Dåvonnå Heckelskein	Medieval Serious	Finance & Accounting (Retail)
3	Daniel Henninger	Old Comics (Flash)	Litigation & Financial Administration
4	Morgan McKenzie	Steam Locomotive	Product Development/Brands Management
5	Rama Abbas Alazantlan	Tribal (Subliminal Eyes)	Clinical Psychology & Lecturer
6	Latisha Valentine Brown	Gossip & PR Effects (Bosch)	HR & Corporate Communications
7	Zalmay Khalizad	Waiting (Hopper)	Commercial R.E. Management
8	Tomas Jesus Gomez	Old Comics (Professor Panel)	Budget & Sales Management
9	Anastasia Longoria	Factory Women	Factory Management (Maquiladoras)
10	Jason Leviathan	Man on Painted Canvas	Client Relations Manager
11	Melaney Ann Saroj	Schematics (Tinguely)	Industrial Designer (Homemaker)
12	Stephan Mlynarczyk	2 Men at Desks (Woodcuts)	Financial Analyst & Day Trader
13	Tunku Varadarajan	Child's Boat Watercolor	Marine Operations Management
14	Eiko Samebelong	Board Reviewing Man (Raune)	Global Corporate Troubleshooter
15	Vladimir Kolesnikov	New York Street (MOMA)	Exporter & Importer
16	Packy Sparkman	Village Church (Hopper)	Senior Management Executive—Asia
17	Penté Pocket	"Empty Pockets" (Staircased)	International Auditor & Examiner
18	Joseph Delmonico	Jockey on Old Car (Magritte)	Senior Oil Analyst
19	Anais Ave Anslak	Stagecoach	Fashion Buyer (Wholesale)
20	Silas Green	Vaudeville Poster/Brick Wall	Chief Marketing Officer
21	Sanjo Catolicá	Cogs & Gears	Space Products Manager
22	Nicanor Duarte Frutos	Equestrian (Lautrec)	Research Manager (Nanolithography)
23	Pédro X. Santiaño	Bus Tickets (Mexico)	Security Specialist (Mexican Ops)
24	Soonja Tree Wajahili	Tahitian Woman (Gauguin)	Pharma Sales Rep
25	Lawrence Kalishnikov	Bride & Bachelor (Duchamp)	Data Systems Design Engineer
26	Mary Kelley O'Brien	Old Handwritten Letter	Customer Service Manager
27	Joseph Washington	Medieval Alchemist	Chemist & Product Design Director
28	Mimi Natasha Baleen	Rabbit in Rabbit (Durer)	Community Relations (Foundations)
29	Warren X. Worthing	Hardened Walls (Armored)	Corporate Security (Shopping Malls)
30	Rosemary Hinman	Church (Hopper)	Wholesale Church Supply Manager

No.	NAME	KEY GRAPHIC THEME	FIELD OF WORK OR EXPERTISE
31	Haixim Li Jinan	Eurasian Worker Art (Panels)	International Logistics Manager
32	Svetiana Vôjinovic	Medieval Portrait	Branding (Guerrilla Marketing)
33	Darien Hollingsworth	Old Comics (Flash Lantern)	Mining Management (Brazil)
34	Marilyn Elaine Vanetti	Old Comics (Crime Panel)	Criminal Behavior Specialist
35	Vladamir Stepan Trofimovitch	Industrial (Duchamp)	Turnaround Specialist (Transnational)
36	Heather Kalinki Chapperwall	Woman at Window (Hopper)	Songwriter & Stage Designer
37	Sigfried Manchak	Rocket Man (Old Newsclip)	Document Control Director
38	Avaña Maria de Gorbari-Estoña	Wonder Woman (Old Comics)	International Licensing Manager
39	Edward James Hopper	Hotel Management (Hopper)	Hotel Management
40	Cathryne Li Li Yang	Wall & Eyes (Michelangelo)	Manager of Shopping Experience
41	Olli Pekka Kalzo	Bluto $$$ (Old Comics)	Spot Market Manager
42	Ankeliki Sonalan	Old Movie Poster (Fear)	Data Storage & FTP Specialist
43	Saud Al-Faisal Abdullah Mitab	Mongolian Traders	International Broker
44	Marcia Anne Turkenov	Hog (Durer)	Marketing & Product Placement
45	Prabhakar Raghavan	Blackboards & Comics	Chief Technology Officer
46	Belinda Staar	Old Comics (Futuristic)	Unstated
47	Karl Van Rue	Old Atlas Tire Ad	Auto Master & Vintage Vendor
48	Marie Selena St. Thomas	Kitchen Scene (Old Painting)	Chef
49	Mark Rothko	Man Showing Shirt (Hopper)	Real Estate Agent
50	John Smith	Printing Room (Medieval)	Print Marketing Director
51	Hazel Anne Hallaghan	Financial Stats (WSJ)	Hedge Fund Manager (Consultant)
52	Roberto Ocala-Jones	Worker Mural (Rivera)	Seminar Promotions (Mexico)
53	Lilliana Belina Muzkow	Worker Mural (Rivera)	AV Events Manager
54	Michael Bineto Zepatone	Old House (Painting)	Death Specialist (Funeral Director)
55	Wendella Moye	Intimate (Modern Art)	Sales Management
56	Vinnie Chang	Chinese Hanging Panels	Office Systems Design
57	Merilee Wellweather	Auto Race (Wind in Willows)	POS Marketing Manager
58	Lord Lee Oxburgh	Rube Goldberg (Fat Man)	Advertising Director
59	Keela Baknevsky	Clock Room (Old Litho)	Controller & Treasurer

No.	NAME	KEY GRAPHIC THEME	FIELD OF WORK OR EXPERTISE
60	Aäge Bjerré	Main Street (Old Photo)	Future Services Planner
61	Sara Robinson	Chinese Fish (Panels)	Telemarketing Management
62	Hwang Woo Suk	Old Car (Sketch)	Process & Design Manager
63	Neikko Nagamine	Winter Snow Scene	Biometric Identifier Specialist
64	Katsuaki Watanabe	International Bank Notes	Corporate Office Park Construction
65	Romano Polynska	Paris Street Scene	Petroleum Fire Manager
66	Rachel Worthington	Woman's Profile	Technology Director/Creative Manager
67	Mark Jones	Superman (Old Comics)	Project Director (International)
68	Nenita Lula Torres	Studio (Matisse)	Audience Animator & Studio Artist
69	Wilson Masingale	Rail Yard (Old Photo)	Manager of Change (Operation Controls)
70	Francis Walswark	Egyptian Farmers	Agronomist & Seed Scientist
71	Mabak Dae Quedo	Reading Room (Painting)	Financial Publishing
72	Ellie Mason-Quinn	Cows in Field (Painting)	Hospital Art Director
73	Waleen Offmann	Man with Bull & Farmer	Advertising Manager (Telecommunications)
74	Dâdi Simcha Perlmuttâr	Huge Factory Gears	Industrial Operations Management
75	Albert Winston Vergé III	Portrait with Car	Industrial Design & Packaging
76	Jovês Mansala	Portrait & Book on Table	Lifestyle Planner & Personal Concierge
77	Felipe Zapata	3-in-1 Man (Masserl)	Secretary to CEO & VIPs
78	Jon Coco Monsini	Men Conferring (Painting)	Software Design/Project Manager
79	Byung Kwon Kim	Old Tractor (Photo)	Director of Supply Chain
80	Yamina Qurina	Factory (Old Litho)	Manufacturing Senior Executive
81	Robert Q. Rathbone	3 Chinese Planters	Manufacturing Team Builder
82	Romando Antonio Lamarez	Old Comics (Flash Running)	Human Resources Management
83	William Prescott Morrow	Man Pondering (Painting)	Counselor & Mental Health Worker
84	Sassoon Luåm Çang Gai	Oriental Carpets	Chief Technical/Conflict Advisor
85	Siento Sanchigora	Chinese Scrolls	Strategy Manager & Business Liaison
86	Luiz Lula Ina del Sallo	Dogs (Drawings)	Merchandising Specialist (Vet Products)
87	Jon Stanos Aûzbeck & Jan Lauren Aûzbeck	Quilted Patterns	Packaging & Marketing (Duo)

No.	NAME	KEY GRAPHIC THEME	FIELD OF WORK OR EXPERTISE
88	Bob Reynolds	Man (Rivera Line Drawing)	Poet & Public Relations Specialist
89	Shaune-X Cartier	Graffiti (Painting)	Communications & Promotions (Music)
90	Ronald Wonfield	Facing Portraits (Lautrec)	Best Practices Manager
91	Hiachi Maguro	Driver (Lautrec)	Real Estate Projects (Global)
92	Noémi Zuazo	Woman in Chair (Painting)	International Model
93	Dieter Zetsche	Portrait (Masserl Woodcut)	European Liaison & Entrepreneur
94	Silas Lapham	Man Swinging Axe (Litho)	Manager & Planner
95	Michelle Wie	Woman with Plume (Painting)	Information Technologist
96	Ernest Block	Man Hammering Anvil	TV Director
97	Lia Rosanatti	Woman in Woman Portrait	Business Manager (Start-ups)
98	Alaña Espirito	Woman Thinking (Painting)	Quality Assurance (Latin America)
99	Alexander William MacIntosh	Civil War Scene (Painting)	Corporate Storyteller
100	Juanito Ruiz Partanenon	Cervantes on Horse	Global Traffic Manager

JOSEPH BALLATINO

1011 WINDING HILLS ROAD
ASHEVILLE, NORTH CAROLINA 66233
TELEPHONE (555) 323-9734
jabaman@gogogoogle.net

CREATIVE CONSTRUCTION
PROJECT DIRECTOR

A *COMMON SENSE* DRIVEN MANAGER
- ✌ Outspoken & Self Reliant
- ✋ Tenacious & Industrious
- ☝ Reliable & Enterprising
- ☜ Stable & Good-Natured
- ☞ Practical & Energized
- ☟ Focused & Forthright
- ✋ Tactful & Instructive

PROJECT WRAPS
- ❖ **VANITY PALACE (1996–99)**
- ❖ **PRIDEMAN'S PLACE (1999–2003)**
- ❖ **PLANTATION VILLAGE (2003–04)**
- ❖ **NO MOSS STONE CONDOS (2004)**
- ❖ **WALMARTWORLDS (2000–Present)**
- ❖ **PLASTIC CITIES (2000–06)**
- ❖ **TOTAL VIAGRA STADIUM (2007–08)**

PEOPLE & MONEY
- ☐ **PROJECTS FROM $220,000,000**
- ● **TRADESPEOPLE FROM 600–1,400**
- ☐ **STEELCLAD ALUM. & CONCRETE FORM**
- ▲ **SKYGARDEN ATRIUMS UP TO 30 STORIES**

Dåvonnå Heckelskein

337 BOULEN 'D COLOGNE #10

KLOTENHOFFEN, DENMARK

CONTACT ONLY VIA NEW YORK AGENT
SKOSEX SSA (212) 727-8859

MANAGING PEOPLE DOESN'T COME NATURALLY TO A LOT OF PEOPLE

BUT IT DOES TO ME

STYLE, PERSONA, WORK ETHIC

RETAIL 20 YEARS WORKING MARGINS

WHOLESALE LONG ENOUGH

TEAM LEADER MAJOR RECENT CHAPTER 11S DUE DILIGENCE

AUTONOMOUS M&A SPREADSHEETER

MBA CPA MEMBERSHIPS

HAVE NOTEWORK WILL TRAVEL RELOCATE NORTHERN HEMISPHERE

HAVE RECENTLY BEEN RENUMERATED BY

HillaryMcCain and **Gore & Gumby** and **Citicorp** and **Dow Jones** and **P&G** and **AliAbba**

HAVE RECENTLY BEEN RECOGNIZED FOR

ascertaining	administering	advising	analyzing	calculating	charting	checking
classifying	collecting	conducted	consolidating	controlling	detailing	determining
directing	dissecting	eliminating	enforcing	establishing	examining	explaining
extracting	federal filing	financing	generating	identifying	inspecting	instituting
interviewing	investigating	negotiating	obtaining	overseeing	projecting	preparing
reporting	reconciling	resolving	reviewing	scheduling	undertaking	weighing

A MORE DETAILED RENDERING OF THE WORKING EVENTS IN A LONG CAREER IS AVAILABLE FROM ME. IN PERSON. CERTAINLY AT YOUR CONVENIENCE. THANK YOU.

Daniel Henninger

MANAGER

MATERIAL ADVERSE CHANGES

Litigation Team Building

ZERO LIABILITY TARGETING

COMPLEX ARBITRATIONS
EXPEDITION SCHEDULES
PANEL PRESENTATIONS
INVESTOR REPRESENTATION
INTERNATIONAL EXCHANGES
MAXI-FUNDS BALANCING
EQUITIES & ANNUITIES
COLLATERALIZATIONS
MSCI INDEX ANALYSIS
EU HUB AVERAGES
KEY CURRENCIES

4558 Maple Street
Suite 1309–B
Worcester, MA 01608
(339) 587–6652
dantheman@flash.net
(888) 882–3864
(339) 688–3975
LifeDisast.Com

MORGAN McKENZIE

When I Get Things Going, All I Can Tell My Competitors Is

"Get Out Of My Way!"

Vice President, Product Development
Link Bellagio Ltd.

Product Marketing Director
PriMedia Hispania SSA

National Brands Manager
GlobalWEBCO.com

Product & New Business Development Manager
Badgley Mischka LLC

288 ELKHORN ROAD
933.228.5566

DELANE, KS 28834
LOCOMAN@SALETRAIN.ORG

TRIBAL COMPREHENSION RUNS DEEP

Rama Abbas Alazantlan

23 CARAVAN TENT TRAIL   VIOLINS, COLORADO 28774   ISLARAMA@PRE2LUDE.COM

Clinical Psychology Lecturer
WITH AN INFORMED & EXTRA-ACADEMIC MUSLIM'S WORLD VIEW

CREATIVE COURSES

Mental Illness & Psychodrama on TV
Gangbanging in Executive Suites
The Baddest Boy Syndrome
Big Boy Toys & Habits of Murderers
Female Mystique & Society of Sex
Uprooted Children in Flight
The Men Gods Fear
Catatonia & Communication Links
Killing Girls in America: Statistical Studies

WORK ENVIRONMENTS

St. Lucy's Asylum – Upstate NY
St. George's Asylum – Lower NJ
Smith Family Sanitorium – The South
Big Goat Ranch Hospital – Mississippi
Gruff & Francie's House – Texas
Singing River Psycho Wards – Iowa

ATTENDANT-IN-CHARGE
Joseph Heller's Big Nut House – Maine
John Updike's Hampton House

PERSONA IN ACTION I
Interned in mental health programs with primary focus on behavior in the clinical wards of state mental hospitals. Provided therapeutic milieus and guidelines as well as new recommendations for state agencies in the Deep South and the Atlantic Seaboard, including Manhattan.

PERSONA IN ACTION II
Founded The Solipsism Institute in the high plains of Colorado to offer meditation and similar eastern philosophies and relaxation techniques to people who are particularly troubled by the large accumulations of money they are in charge of and cannot reasonably account for other than good luck.

Latisha Valentine Brown

c/o THE MORNINGLORY CENTER
1200 AVENUE OF THE ANGELS
LOS ANGELES, CALIFORNIA 99999
latishafish@moonlink.net

MISINFORMING RUMORMONGERS CAN BE RUINOUS

CAN YOUR BUSINESS **AFFORD** THE LUXURY OF BLIND ESCAPE?

Is dissension amongst your ranks undermining service & quality?

I am a resourceful troubleshooter who can spark creative energies in workplaces where exciting ideas are rewarded fairly. If innovation and experimenting are critical to your company, you should talk to me. Weaving leading edge concepts into existing complex situations is one of my particular specialties—connecting the dots between people and technologies. I gain the support of managers and team leaders through participative decision making, sharing key knowledge openly, encouraging employees to commit to their highest potential, and by addressing the most crucial issues that have historically broken down the company's communication life-lines.

MOST CHALLENGING WORK	WHO & WHERE & WHEN	WHY & WHAT ESSENTIALLY HAPPENED
♣ **Employee Incentives** *Putting something on the table.*	**AMTEX (Mumai 02 & 06)** **HOTEL & RESORT OWNERS**	Restore eroding customer loyalty. *Established aura of competition to win.*
♣ **Employee Services** *Trading out for gainsharing.*	**CITO (LAS VEGAS 03–05)** **HOTEL & CASINO OWNERS**	Spiralling benefits & compensation. *Pegged worker trade-offs to performance.*
♣ **Force Restructuring** *Creating a sense of order.*	**RuPee (Singapore 00–01)** **HOTEL & RACETRACK OWNERS**	Improved "reaction team" building. *Flying work-wedges applied to group goals.*
♣ **Plant Stratification** *Fixing a flattened command.*	**Nucor (US/Europe 98-00)** **GLOBAL STEEL PRODUCER**	Reorganizing tiers for better controls. *Strong units with clear paramenters.*
♣ **Coordinating Operations** *Remote multi disconnects.*	**Gordon LLC (NY 97-98)** **INTERNATIONAL MANUFACTURING**	Cost cutting and defining. *Designated native-based foreign liaisons.*
♣ **Public Relations** *Media reshaping brands.*	**ParisH (LA 92-94)** **LICENSOR & DISTRIBUTOR**	Negative brand identification (news). *Media placements of products (sitcoms).*

BEST LEARNING EXPERIENCES

* **NY School of Social Research (M.A., Philosophy); Fashion Institute of Technology off-site studies in new textile technology; "Crafting Communication" seminars with top European & West African business leaders.**

CHICAGO

3400 LAKE AVENUE

Day Telephone

288.988.4100

Night Messages

288.383.2074

zak@shopmall.net

ZALMAY "BUDDY-0" KHALIZAD

WASHINGTON

1290 JEFFERSON DR.

Day Telephone

922.1096.3345

Night Messages

922.555.7832

zak@mallshops.com

Shops & Malls

FLORIDA

SAILBOAT PLAZA

5.5 CAP, AAA

BOCA RATON

OCEANVIEW

7.84 CAP, NNN

NAPLES

SHARK CITY

7.59 CAP, $87/sf

MIAMI

Properties & Investments

Commercial Managing Director

Marcus & Millichamp

FLORIDA & CALIFORNIA REGIONS

20+ Years

Extraordinary Results

A Market Maker

Net-Lease

CALIFORNIA

CAMBRIDGE TOWER

7.4 CAP, NEAR NASA

CANOGA PARK

APPLETON SKY

6 CAP, NNN LEASE

SAN DIEGO

SILICON FLAGSHIP

4.33 CAP, UPTOWN

ALAMEDA

IF YOU'RE WATCHING THE HORIZON, YOU MIGHT SEE ME COMING

I am not so laid back

that I forget where I am or nod off

when investors plow through the numbers,

but I am relaxed when the big money is on the table

and somebody's got to do something to make it all happen.

WAITING FOR CLIENTS TO SHOW UP WON'T BUMP UP LEASING RATES

TOMAS JESUS GOMEZ

TROUBLESHOOTER

10 Dirty Dusty Road/Alta, OK 44312/800.923.2230

BUDGET MANAGEMENT

Project Design
Field Audits
Staff Development
Hiring & Firing
Qualitative Testing

S & M MANAGEMENT

Pricing Strategies
POS Leads
District Incentives
Channels & Tiers
QT-QA Testing

BITS & BYTES

2003 TO THE PRESENT
SVP Sales
VP Marketing
Outsource Director
Insource Planner

2000 TO 2003
Director,
International Sales

1996 TO 2000
VP National Sales
Marketing Manager

CLOSE ENCOUNTERS OF THE UNKIND

THE RELATIVITY CORPORATION ▲ CHICAGO & L.A.

Principal spearhead for the massive M&A transition when TRC purchased Altion Software and merged 9 business units, 3 of which were profit centers. The results are well-known, as is my role in making it all happen within their threshold windows. It was in fact my leadership that led to the spin-off of failing assets.

DISCOVER SPACE LTD. ▲ BIRMINGHAM & SAN FRANCISCO

Major innovator who introduced new channeling and distribution systems for space industry products and support systems, which are the most lucrative parts of the convoluted contracts.

ELYSIAN FIELDS INC. ▲ SALT LAKE CITY

A VC firm troubleshooter who becomes the in-house expert on foreign funeral home supplier networks. Big money made here.

WHEN I PRY UNDER A ROCK TO SEE WHAT'S THERE, I PACK A GUN.

ANASTASIA LONGORIA

No. 9 Ranchos de Verdes
Santa Maria, D.R.
longoria@dominican.org

MANUFACTURING OPERATIONS VICE PRESIDENT

OPERATIONS SYSTEMS • STRATEGIC PLANNING • COST MANAGEMENT • FEDERAL EPA
HR COMPLIANCE • OFFSHORE PRODUCTION • QA/QC • UNION & LABOR RELATIONS
INTERLINKED FACILITIES DESIGNS & CONTROLS • INTL. DISTRIBUTION • OUTSOURCING

FACTORY WORK & MY SUCCESS

My successful achievements are the result of choosing the right partners. My decision making has been on the mark 99% of the time because I didn't cut corners and I enlisted the aid of dedicated and knowledgeable workers.

I share with the people who deserve to know the whole plan, and hold back distracting information from those who wouldn't know how to use it properly. I act on instinct and intelligence rather than wait for the "what" that others look to save them, and as a result of taking action, I have been able to foresee disasterous consequences of others' actions based on consensus.

I have made tough decisions by standing up for principles which were not always widely supported, but in the long run proved to be valuable and beneficial to our shareholders.

MANUFACTURING TEXAS/MEXICO

Maquiladoras
Reporting
INS Permits
Work Papers
Police Issues
Supply Chains
Federal XPS
Customs

CORPORATE EMPLOYERS CORPORATE CONTRACTORS

TEXAMERICANA PRODUCTS CORP.

VP MANUFACTURING $30M Y-E PROJECTED
VP/GM MANUFACTURING $21–28M 02-06
GM/OPERATIONS $13M 00-02

TRANSMEX INTERNATIONAL INC.

GM PLANT STARTUP (MONTERREY) 98-00
MFG MGR/INVENTORY SYSTEMS 94-98

LOUGHLIN & LARAMIE INVESTMENT CORP.
AUSTEX IMPORT CORP.
PLANT CONSULTING & TROUBLESHOOTING
LABOR POOL MANAGEMENT & EQUIPMENT CONTROL

DO YOU EVER FEEL LIKE YOU ARE
NOTHING MORE THAN
PAINT ON CANVAS?

2005–06
CZECH REPUBLIC
LEHMAN BROS.
ANDERSEN NOR

1994–2000
LITHUANIA
OAKLEY GARDE
TELSTRA TELFONE

1997–2001
CYPRUS
CAMELBACK & CO.
BARCLAYS PLC

2000–04
SLOVAKIA
AUXIETTE PLC
DEUTSCHE BANK

2002–03
MALTA
KAZAKHSTANKO

JASON LEVIATHAN
CLIENT RELATIONS MANAGER

I BUILD TRUST, MORE THAN MONEY

1999–2001
SLOVENIA
DELA LORIE
MACKAY PLC

No. 39 · Besoldungrüppe
Amt für Züsasford, Belgium
hardman@moneypit.com

1995, 2000
POLAND
WELLS JEFCO
SUPRASTAR

MELANEY ANN SAROJ

10 East Hillside Boulevard
Countryside, Minnesota 22010
TELEPHONE 555-345-2755
CELLPHONE 205-666-0099
EMAIL GEARWORKS@WORK.NET
WEBSITE CHAPLINSCLOCK.ORG

INDUSTRIAL DESIGNER WITH HOUSEHOLD EXPERIENCE

Housewife turned industrial engineer after ten years of homelife experience as a result of faulty electronic products and misengineered appliances. BSE from state university with additional studies at Northrup Grumman/Lockheed Martin joint venture programs. Equally adept in Autocad & prototype modeling.

Good problem solver with the patience gained from rearing wonderful children. Excellent common sense despite what my husband thinks. Able to weave concepts into existing R&D. I understand complex programs and long-term goals while working at the same time on tonight's grocery list. I operate on a deep faith through difficult personal and business challenges, and usually can effortlessly gain support of my coworkers to share their important views and critical ideas.

I have a true conviction to principles and a genuine commitment to attainable excellence in all endeavors.

I willingly accept Change as the underlying 'heat-core' nature of engineering and I am not afraid to defend my team's vision.

I possess the personal drive to sell ideas as exciting to others.

A stand-up teacher and stand-beside mentor.

PORTFOLIO & TRACK RECORD AVAILABLE

By the way, I own 11 patents, and have 6 pending.

STEPHAN MLYNARCZYK

POST OFFICE BOX 7899   GRAND MARINA, CAYMAN ISLANDS

CONTACT: BANK OF ENGLAND ROYAL DUTCH OFFICE 01.033.925.3488 #8

FINANCIAL ANALYST
END-OF-LIFE PLANNER
DAY TRADER

ANNUITIES/FOREIGN ACCOUNTS/SWISS BANKS/CURRENCY CONVERSIONS

Exceptional Asset Manager

Master of Capital Market & VC Funds

Entrepreneurial Startup Investments Liaison

CREATIVE INVESTMENT STRATEGIES SINCE 1980.

FORMER MORGAN BROKER & FLOOR MANAGER.

BROAD KNOWLEDGE OF HI-TECH & NASDAQ.

MARKET PARTNERS IN HONG KONG & BANGKOK.

SOLID "STREET" REPUTATION WITH HEDGE FUND MANAGERS

Compliance & Regulatory Series 7 & 24 Registrations

Upper Crust Business Schools & Credentials

BIOBLOG BIODATA

I am a kind and gentle man who has a wealth of financial knowledge in foreign and domestic markets. I believe I am considerate and accommodating, empathetic to legal and moral dilemmas my clients find themselves in, and possess an agreeable and circumspect nature. In business, I always aim to be ethical and principled, and in judgments, impartial and receptive to counsel of the interested parties.

CLIENT LIST SINCE 1980

DUPONT

MAYTAG SO-AM

KLEIN SSA

DERGUSSENSTATT

HONEYWELL

PACIFIC INDUSTRIES

KAYPRO KELLERMAN

ART INDUSTRIES LLC

BAPTIST MISSIONS CO.

BAVARIAN BREWERIES

ASTON MARTIN

POWER YACHT CORP.

FLOATING HOTELS

SKY CASINOS LTD.

for a thorough review of my recent writings in journals go to

$$$GROW.COM

ASK FOR AL

THE ESTABLISHMENT & I

- ◆ ShearsonBurnsWatson 2003–05
- ◆ Morgan Stanley 1998–2003
- ◆ Greenburg Money Markets 2000
- ◆ Fannie Mae Consulting 2000-04
- ◆ Freddie Mac Consulting 1980-90
- ◆ Resolution Trust Chairman 1983
- ◆ Bond Trader & Hedge Manager
- ◆ Day Trader & Risk Analyst

Tunku Varadarajan

MARINE OPERATIONS

bigboysboat@navigator.net

3009 Isla del las Rosaritos
No. 444 Playas y Pendajos
Ziaxentienatico Sur, Ecuador
Telephone 01 (20) 9933–7766

I RUN THE SHIP
BECAUSE I STEERED THE BOAT
THROUGH SEAS OF DOLLARS

SAVVY & RESOURCEFUL EX-MARINE EX-HARBOR PILOT WITH EXTENSIVE GLOBAL ROUTE SHIPPING BACKGROUND WHO KNOWS HOW TO UNPLUG BOTTLENECKS AND NEGOTIATE BETWEEN NASTY-TEMPERED GREEK MAGNATES AND SNARLING HARDHEADED EASTERN BLOCK CAPTAINS WHO RUN THINGS THEIR OLD WAYS.

PartnerShips Are EVERYTHING On the HIGH SEAS

I *control* my crew's concerns by designating "who does what."
I *learn* from group intelligence and their consensus view.
I *reduce* mistakes by communicating my "do this first."
I *provide* leadership through unquestioned decisions.
I *find* a team's strongest for my best allies & leaders.

SHIPPING LANES

2003-05	LEXO LINES/THE SWEDISH SSA	"Mon Amor"
2001-03	HEIDELBERG BONNON LINES	"Stuttengartt"
2000-01	CRUISE PACIFIC LINES/ASIAN-X	"Flower Wild"
1994-00	GRAND CAYMAN LINES LLC	"Temptress 2"
1992-94	BRISTOL SEASIDE ISLAND LINES	"Banana King"
1980-92	JAMAICAN TRANSNATIONAL INC.	"Mamo Jumbi"

EIKO SAMEBELONG

909 Relevance Avenue
Kingsland, Texas 78639
(325) 828-4444

"COMMUNICATE"

See Man work & play.
See Man talk & listen.

[LISTEN]

I CAN
**COLLABORATE
COMMUNICATE
CREATE**

signs & symbols

I SPEAK LANGUAGES.
- ENGLISH TO PORTUGUESE
- FRENCH TO ENGLISH
- MANAGEMENT TO MFG.
- MARKETING TO SALES

I PAINT PICTURES.
- GLOBAL MARKET LANDSCAPES.
- PUBLIC RELATIONS STRATEGIES.
- CROSS CULTURAL BRANDING.

I TAKE TRIPS.
- ASIAN MANUFACTURING.
- EUROPEAN ACQUISITIONS.
- SOUTH AMERICAN SOURCES.

I BRING.
- CREATIVE PERSPECTIVES.
- VISUALIZED OPPORTUNITIES.
- MATERIALIZED RESULTS.

global & national

I SPEND TO SAVE. My employers pay me to go to far-flung places and see what the trouble is. They expect me to keep my head on my shoulders and find work-throughs to problems that can cost a fortune before anyone even knows it. I am extremely good at this because I know how to do some things exceedingly well:
- explaining circumstances diplomatically
- twisting arms to counter resistance
- calling bluffs (language excuses; laziness)
- providing initiatives and rewards
- demanding broad accountability

My colleagues at the companies below, where I worked, will back up my claims:
- **BROADWAY BRANDS LLC** (2004-06)
- **China Central GlobeEX+** (2001-04)
- **WestMeetsEast Ltd.** (1998-01)
- **Corazonas Alturon SSA** (1986-96)

VLADIMIR KOLESNIKOV

EXPORTER TENACIOUS & COMPETITIVE IMPORTER

DIPLOMATIC & FORTHRIGHT & OPTIMISTIC & PERSISTENT
Bold & Accommodating & Cooperative & Obliging & Facilitating
Enterprising & Industrious & Practical & Positive & Tactful & Energized

TRANSNATIONALS

RUNA PURNOMOSA S.A.

JAKARTA JADE INVESTORS

MAHATHIR MOHAMAD INC.

KUALA LUMPUR HIHO LTD.

PROTON HOLDINGS BHD.

FU CHENGYU CHINACOAST

IVAN CHUNG DIRECTIONS

CREDIT RATINGS XINHUA

SHANGHAI FINANCE CORP.

GULER SABANCI & STEED

SABANCI HOLDING CO.

KEMALAN–ATATURK BHD.

IGNACIO BUNYE

ARROYO PETUKHOV COS.

TENGKU MAHALEEL ARIFF

MENGISTU HAILE MARIAM LEG-
WAILA LEGWAILA LLC.

NEVZLIN YUKOS

TRINKETS & BABBLES CO.

3RD WORLD BOZOS.COM

DEAFENING SILENCE COS.

INTERNATIONAL MANAGEMENT

CAPITAL INVESTMENTS & FINANCING

- ◆ Double-Hulled SOS Cargo Ships
- ◆ Level–VII Secure Container Systems
- ◆ UNIVERS–XTRAK Routing Management
- ◆ Sub-electronics (Indonesia; Malaysia; Surinam)
- ◆ Market Commodities (Bulk Grains: North Africa)
- ◆ Transhipped Key Components (Interfax)
- ◆ 30-Year Term Leasing & Refinancing
- ◆ Export Portfolios & Global VC/XPOs

MOHAMADAN & PROTON HOLDINGS BHD.

- ◆ Outsourced Assembled Units (GM; Daimler)
- ◆ Insourced Subassembled Units (Nissan; Renault)

FU CHENGYU & CHUNG/SHANGHAI LTD.

- ◆ China Republic Armament
- ◆ Libyan Stockpile Transfers (UN Watchgroup)
- ◆ Cuba–Venezuela & Peru–Cuba Trades

ATATURK & TENGKU & ABBAS MAHOUD

- ◆ Textiles & Manufacturing Equipment
- ◆ Consumables & Distribution Equipment

Portfolio & Spreadsheets
russiankoly@worldtrade.com

NO. 1 NEFTEYUGANSK PLACE • NEW YORK, NY 10007 • 212.322.5572

Packy Sparkman

FLAT A, 55/B ORCHID COURT
KOWLOON, HONG KONG

YANG LEE ROAD, LEE CITY
535.399.2228/PACKY@KAA.NET

A Man of the Moment

creative, inspired, teaching and leading

a planner who follows through thoroughly

financially astute and socially stable

comfortable amdist chaos of transitions

SENIOR MANAGEMENT EXECUTIVE

speaking fluent English, Cantonese, Mandarin
and German, with fair Russian (in the works).
I carefully maintain a global network of important
Indonesian and Indian corporate executive
contacts through the my alumni network.
I opened up new markets through successful
representation and negotiation with national
and regional governments at the ministerial
and regulatory body levels. Full P&L charge
of region generating $390m euros working with
Big 6 auditors in East Asia division revamping.
Recruited as turnaround agent for EU cos.

2006—Now
WANG INTERNATIONAL
HONG KONG OFFICE

2003—2006
ASIAN PACIFICA CORP.
NEW ZEALAND

2000—2003
SAB MILLER GRUPO
BRAZIL

1996—2000
BBVA SOVEREIGN
SEOUL, SK

1990, 1994
BBA, MBA
UCLA

I have been looking into people's pockets for about 20 years and I am always amazed at 2 things: What I find, and what is gone missing. Because I am a person who is unafraid to take on the unpleasant task of audit autopsies, I can offer a challenging company both intellectual depth and emotional intelligence, forged from experience in a range of industrial organizations, and equally fine tuned by academic training at the finest of educational institutions in Europe. I also have learned to articulate strategic visions in a fluent manner so my assistants can gather what is relevant and what is not.

I have continually demonstrated my ability to make judgments that are wholly based on verifiable facts, and I have a vast track record of being creative and level-headed when it comes to dealing with extremely complex and complicated financial problems.

I am strong but kind and gentle, and I very much enjoy my work; I can also get the job done on the target and on budget.

I know how to listen as well as talk, learn, teach, grow and perceive.

SENIOR OIL ANALYST

Joseph Delmonico

21 Bedford Road East
Toronoto, Ontario
Canada M5R 2J9
gusher.godeep@oil.org

טק נזג ללב פי וצבט ןקוד ןי לין.

ı̆ǎ̆ε̆ ε̆ı̆ı̆ı̆η φı̆φ ı̆ı̆¨ ´ı̆ ´ı̆η̂ı̆ ε̆¨ı̆

МЦФИПР КШОЛ ДЬТЩЗЫ ЪЙГК

سصخرسخزشر دشخ شرخصخصسذ٤ص تتإ٥أش دذش

International Experience
I Like to Be the First
AND MORE OFTEN THAN NOT
I Usually Am

2000 to Present
International Energy Agency (PARIS)

The IEA is an international agency committed to the security of the world's energy supply, economic growth, and environmental sustainability through energy policy and understanding among 30 market democracies and advanced resource economics.

BROAD oil industry expertise and knowledge of refining processes and analyses of local and global networked markets. Policymaking experience as well as quantitative analysis skills; adept and flexible in developing analytical methodologies.

FLUENT in working with large databases and interwoven spreadsheets, and able to draft recommendations in English, French, German or Latvian. Possess the insight and understanding of the nature of economic, social, demographic and cultural dimensions of issues and concerns of importance about the future of markets.

DEEP statistical understanding of the sources and uses of statistics as well as demonstrated project team leadership experience. Able to command credibility at home and abroad with a strong track record of introducing and managing change without compromising quality and delivering (and developing) long-term strategies.

SUCCESSFUL experience working within a geographically dispersed organization; proven ability to educate and the stature to influence others on a path to profitable results; know how to properly mobilise resources; able to play a key role in consolidating new management structures; and can develop new system frameworks for db managing.

I LIKE OIL. No, I love oil. No, better yet, I *appreciate* oil. I am a person who faces facts, both personally and professionally. You could call me a Realist. You could call me a Pragmatist. Or, you could just call me: 888.799.3320. I am like a database archaeologist. I like to dig. I like to catalog. I like specimens nicely boxed in spiffy glass cases. That's one side of me. I also like to play rugby and belong to a local rowing team and spend my vacations in the deepest canyons I can find my way out of. It's fun. Creativity is the key to my enduring success. Yours?

ANAIS AVE ANSLAK

WRO—1010.1.01   P.O. BOX CH—4002

BASEL, SWITZERLAND   TEL +41 (0)61 323 79 26

A FASHIONABLE LADY WITH A PAST	A WOMAN WHO CAN FASHION A FUTURE
2005 - PRESENT	2004
LONDON AMERICAN FASHIONS LTD.	**BACHELOR OF MERCHANT SCIENCE**
GLOBAL MERCHANDISE BUYER	LONDON SCHOOL OF ECONOMICS
REPORT DIRECTLY TO VP INTERNATIONAL SALES	*Valedictorian & Highest Honors Graduate*
Wholesale & Retail Fashion Merchandising	*Master Course: Wholesale & Retail Trades*
Merchandising & Systems Strategies	*Merchandising & Information Databases*

what I look for
before I buy & why

I want to know if this is a day or a nite thing. Will it last more than a year?
What will likely come after it? Will it spin off replicas or wannabes?
Is this global or local, and will it cross international borderlines?
Because fashion products are profiles of women & their personas and
reflect the moods of consumers who buy them, looking for meaning in
the signs & symbols found in style, cloth, texture and color is sensible.

⚜

About Me

*I am an artist. That's my creative core, where I start, what I work from
the moment I open my eyes in the morning. My childhood was spent in Rhodesia
on a farm, and I worked in Johannesburg in my early career as an assistant and
financial secretary to a major international exporter. My interest in fashion was
sparked by a job in J-berg with JETBLACKWEAR in Basel which sold Afrikaan
batishkas from colorful remnants in the growing European market. Since then I
have worked for TRIBEX, NAMIBIA TEXTILES, AFRIKAAN SOUL and others.*

UP AGAINST A BRICK WALL?
SILAS GREEN
A Real Show Stopper

I have learned that excess marketing capability is unrelated to the direct size of success; smaller may actually be better in some subsidiary operations.

MFA BOSTON UNIVERSITY 84
MBA INTL MARKETS B.U. 96

M&A ANALYST   MORNINGSTAR 99
SALES DIRECTOR   TRANSCRYPT INTL. 02
PORTFOLIO MARKETING   WILSON & CO. LTD. 04

"I think the Long Hours that my Hard Work often requires should Be Creative Ones too."

DIRECTOR OF CLIENT RELATIONS & CHIEF MARKETING OFFICER
(05 to Now)
THE GLOBE FEDERATION
LONDON/DAKAR/THE HAGUE

CUTTING EDGE TECHNOLOGIES
EURO TRADING RISK ANALYSES
CUSTOMS & BORDER BREAKDOWNS
COMMERCIAL ENTREPRENEURING
FOREIGN ENERGY & COST ISSUES
ORACLE & DB MANAGEMENT
COMMODITY (EU) VALUE-ADDING
LICENSING RENEWALS (EURO)
3- & 5-YEAR COMMITMENT PLANS
STRATEGIC MARKET REVERSALS
STAKEHOLDER RELATIONS
VC & BANKING LIAISON

52 rue Mohamed Alwar
BP 430 Dakar
Dakjar – Senegal
U.S. Tel. 212.849.7841
indgame@showgoon.com

Sanjo Catolicá

400 WEST FOURTH STREET
NEW YORK, NY 10010

212.883.2996

212.550.9329

spacejo@extra-net.org

SPACE Products Manager

EMPLOYERS SINCE 1980

BORDERSPACE GROUP

ALIENSHIP PARTNERS

GODSMARK INTL.

GOMAKE & STAY LTD.

THE SPACETALK CO.

ROSETTO/STONE

MY RECORD
CORPORATE TITLES

Product Development Manager
New Market Research Manager
Product Profiling Manager
Design & Packaging Manager
Market & Sales Manager

SUMMARY

Over the many years of my working with other professionals in this business, I have gained insights and contacts that are unmatchable by other candidates. I not only know how to open the doors to otherwise closed opportunities, but I have hands-on expertise in the labyrinthine process of marketing to this changing industry from year to year. My best success has been with:

Visi-Glow® Tefroglas

DigitronDN® Instrumentations

LabLife® Science Tools

KolpakSTAR® Storage Systems

TIMELINE–RS® Utilities

FreeFlow® Communications

HoloGraphX® Displays

Nicanor Duarte Frutos

174 bd Saint-Germain
75006 Paris
+33 1 45 44 87 43

"Kirungii" Ring Road, Westlands
POB 40092 00100 Nairobi
nano@nano.co.ke

Via dei Roccettiini 9
20 San Domenico di Fiesole
nanotech@rothschild.eu.it

Nanolithography Research Planning Director

THE RACE FOR SMALLER IS ON
FASTER IS HARD TO DEFINE
SMALLER IS HARD TO FIND

PROJECT & POSITIONS
Since 2004

DIRECTOR OF RESEARCH

INFORMATION CONTROL MANAGER

GLOBAL INTEGRATION MANAGER

INVENT–LITH

International Venture Team for Global Research in Applied Nanolithography

INVENT–LITH IS A JOINT VENTURE

International Business Machines

Advanced Micro Devices

Infineon Technologies Ag

MicroTechTools SSA

ASML Holding AV/Albany

PRIMARY FOCUS TO 2010
Lithography Immersion Tools
EUV
Extreme Ultraviolet Lithography
[to 22 nanometers]

CREDENTIALS
Since 1988

R&D DIRECTOR/UNMIK INTL., 2000–2004

I.T. COMMUNICATIONS DIRECTOR
BAVARIAN SWITZERLAND SSA, 1996–2000

BUSINESS DEVELOPMENT MANAGER
RESEARCH & MARKET MANAGER
PRODUCT DEVELOPMENT SCIENTIST
R&D SCIENTIST – BIOGENETICS
KENYAN PRODUCTS LLC, 1988–1996

Curriculum Vitae, Europe

London Business School MBA 1988
University of Cape Town Since 1998

Pricing Strategies & Tactics

Negotiation Strategies for Managers

Integrated Marketing Communications

Leading High–Impact Knowledge Teams

New Strategies for Value Creation

Talented Human Resource Strategies

Transforming Organizations

Policy Making Tools & Techniques

Information Disbursement Tactics

Pédro X. Santiaño

903 Camino Estrellas A202
Colonia Independencia Norte
Guadalajara, Jalisco
MEXICO

pedrox_safe@securidades.net

SECURITY SPECIALIST

Corporate Protection
Corporate Threat Analysis
Emergency Management
Bilingual Contracts Liaison

THE ART OF INFORMATION WARFARE

"2400 years ago Sun Tzu stressed the importance of gathering information in a battle. From the military to local governments, information has never been a more crucial asset. We don't know anyone who develops better security solutions to ensure corporate protection than the old warrior, Señor Santiaño."

— Quoted from *Mexico DF Business Hoy* (2005)

I DELIVER

DOMINANCE THROUGH FORESIGHT

THREAT ANALYSIS

- Determine vulnerable targets for focus.
- Decide which CorpPlan will work best.
- Delegate managers to engage CP Phase 1.
- Deflect infiltrations via CP/IT Phase 1.

EMERGENCY MANAGEMENT

- Coordinate "External Culpables" strategy.
- Evaluate Phase 3 training competencies.
- Ramp up Phases 2–5 'Standard Bearers'.

CORPORATE PROTECTION

- Preventative Plan A: pre-Lockdown Mode.
- Preventative Plan B: Lockdown Mode.
- Reboot Plan A: CleanSweep Mode.
- Wraparound Plan A: Secure Guide Mode.
- Future Protect Plan A: Dot-Connect Plan.

COMPANIES I HAVE PROTECTED FROM HACKERS & BAD GUYS

2003 – PRESENT

PEMEX PETROGASAS
CANTARIAS USA
CEMENTO GLOBO SSA
KPGM FINANCIAL
KENYAN MINING LTD.

2000 – 2003

SYNGENTA
CIGAR SCIONS GROUP
INTL. LIVESTOCK CO.
SULTANATE OF OMAN
THE GRM GROUP
WALDHAUS SILS

1995 – 2000

MEXICO VISION 21
WORLDSHARE
BIOSTIMULATION INC.
SPRINT & SWISS CSAV
AUSTROLEX
IMD INTERNATIONAL
QRIO ROBOTICS
LASER ITALIA

1985 Beach Avenue South A-44
Boca Raton, Florida 33445
(561) 386-3598 Home PM
(211) 780-4452 Cell 24/7
(866) 393-5000 Messages

lakali@duchamp.org

SENIOR
DATA
SYSTEMS
DESIGN
ENGINEER

TICK Tock TICK Tock
RAT-A-TAT-TAT-TAT
ARREEGGA, ARREEGGA
Ka-thump, ka-thump

THE OLD SOUNDS OF
ELECTRONIC SILENCE

NOW MACHINE
ELECTROLYTES
SPEED SILENTLY
ALONG AT WORK

LAWRENCE
KALISHNIKOV

I DO DATA. REALLY FAST DATA

3328 Purple Martin Boulevard
Cape Fear, Missouri 28845
(873) 229-2286

Dear Somebody, Sometime

This missive is about me but it is directed to you, at you, and for you, so it is probably as much about you as it is about me. I do many things well, but one in particular is to oversee personalized customer service.

"A <u>NATURAL</u> FOR CUSTOMER SERVICE"

That's what my friends and peers say about me. Why? Perhaps because my style is pleasant and I'm not easily rattled, because I am creative in dynamic ways when it comes to solving problems.

<u>SOLVE THEM LIKE THEY'RE YOUR OWN</u>

This is my essential philosophy. It works. It could work for you, too.

IT <u>COULD</u> <u>WORK</u> FOR YOU.

If I worked for you, I would probably do better than what you are used to expecting. I always do. I can usually find a way to do the job better. It's just part of me, my innovative personality.

I SMILE BECAUSE I ENJOY MAKING PEOPLE HAPPY.
IT JUST HAPPENS TO MAKE ME HAPPY AS WELL. THAT'S ME.

How about you? What makes you happy? Superior service?

Sincerely (yours),

Mary Kelley O'Brien

irish-setter@thecape.net

Joseph Washington, Ph.D.

DESIGN DIRECTOR
CHEMICAL PRODUCTS INNOVATION

MODERN ALCHEMIST
NANOEXPLORER
MIXOCOLOGIST
PROBING PURIST

VAST CREDENTIALS, ACADEMIC & COMMERCIAL.

8 Maple Lane   Greenville, NC 33882   404.228.5576   drjoe@logos.net

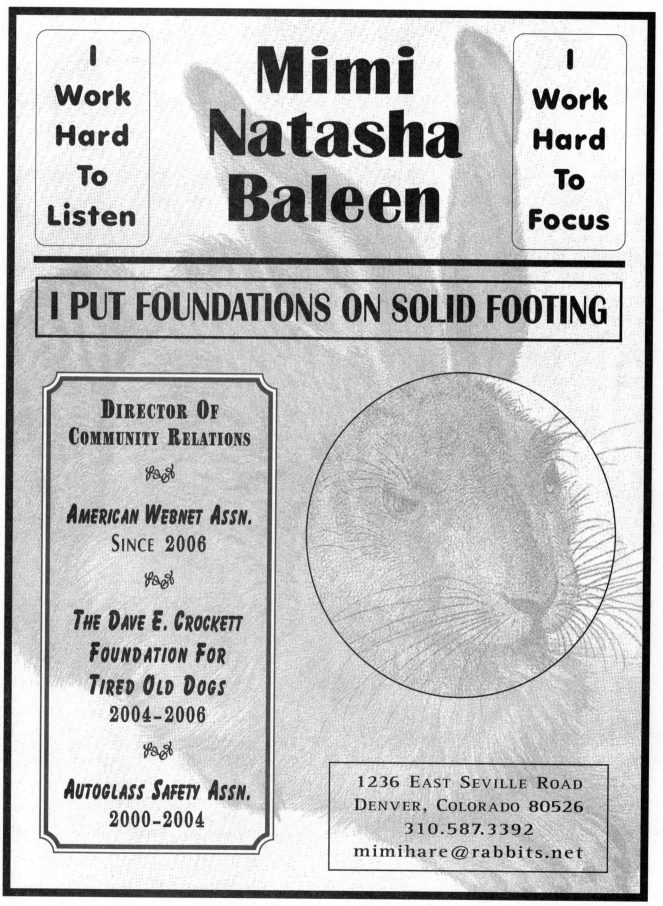

I Work Hard To Listen

Mimi Natasha Baleen

I Work Hard To Focus

I PUT FOUNDATIONS ON SOLID FOOTING

DIRECTOR OF COMMUNITY RELATIONS

❧

AMERICAN WEBNET ASSN.
SINCE 2006

❧

THE DAVE E. CROCKETT FOUNDATION FOR TIRED OLD DOGS
2004–2006

❧

AUTOGLASS SAFETY ASSN.
2000–2004

1236 EAST SEVILLE ROAD
DENVER, COLORADO 80526
310.587.3392
mimihare@rabbits.net

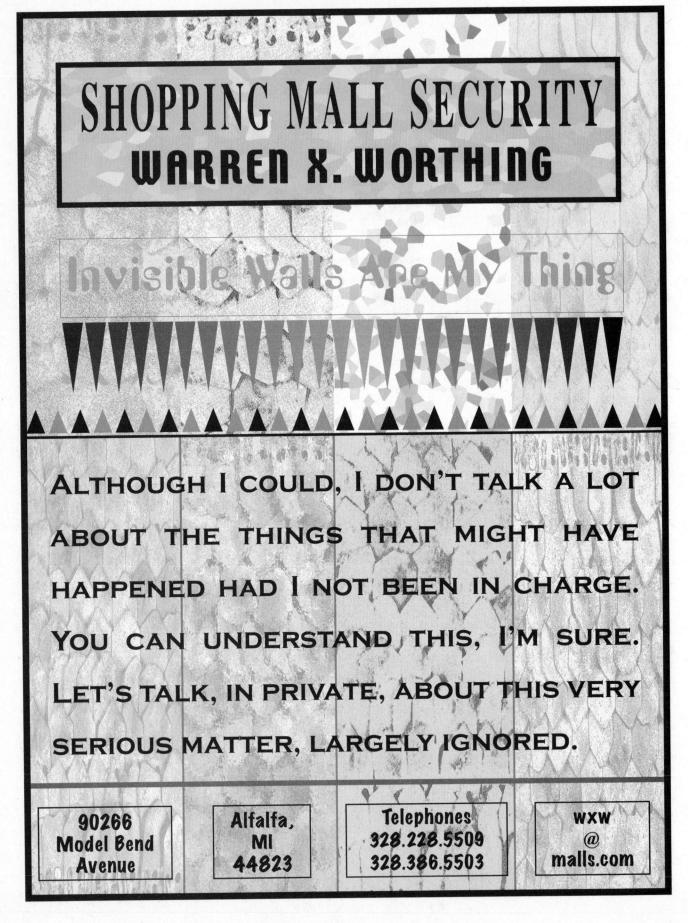

Rosemary 'Queenie' Hinman

Wholesale Church Supply

I know this growing industry from the inside out, with an ever-expanding network of Christian business contacts comprised of purchase managers and other decision-making officials.

NATIONWIDE RELATIONS WITH LEADERS OF
Pentecostal Assemblies
Protestant Associations
Religious Publishers
Group & Club Newsletters
Conventions & Retreats

28 GREAT ROCK PLACE ♥ CAPE MAY, NEW JERSEY 32889 ♥ 888.337.3579

HAIXIM LI JINAN

26 Nefertiti Place ✻ Cairo, Egypt ✻ egypto@archeo-tut-eg.com

A HOUSING LOGISTICS MANAGER
WHO CAN GET YOUR HOUSE IN ORDER
FROM TOP TO BOTTOM, WALL TO WALL, SPIC AND SPAN

HOUSING MASTER

Egypt 2005–c.2007
Gatar & Oman 2004–2005
Libya & Niger 2001–2004
Saudi Arabia 2000–2002
South Africa 1996–2000
Namibia 1992–1996

CONTRACTS
AND CONTACTS

HALLIBURTON
Mssrs Scranton & O'Dell

BLACKSTONE
Mssrs Brendt & Donell

GLOBAL MINING
Mssrs Kyzakoft & Roma

STONES UNLIMITED
Mssrs Bille & Barton

REDWING INTL.
Mssrs Conde & Salanto

LOGISTICS MASTER

Employees & Nations

Egypt 700
Gatar & Oman 1850
Liberia & Niger 620
Saudi Arabia 950–1540
South Africa 425
Namibia 300–630

LOGISTICS

Location Evaluation
On-Site Planning
Land Acquisitions
Major Construction
Temporary/Permanent
Communications
Food & Beverages
Technology & IT
Housing & Sanitation
Transport Systems
Recreation & Mail

GUERILLA MARKETING

Dear Reader,

There is more to brand identification than meets the eye, and brand loyalty is sincerely in the eyes of the brand beholder, which can be a very serious problem that I know how to solve.

My experience in modern marketing (no castles in the air, this) and kingdoms of promoting consumer goods, professional services, media buys and major advertising makes me one of the most versatile and thoughtful candidates who will gaze upon your door. Call.

I dare say you shant regret it.

A WOMAN'S NATURAL MYSTIQUE IS WHAT MAKES HER BUY

SVETIANA VÔJINOVIC

163 Wenheissen Strasse   Dornläap, New Zealand

Connecticut Telephone 232.338.6995   svetiana@denti.org

A LIGHT IN THE DARK

COMPANHIA VALE DO RIO DOCE

BRAZIL MEGACOMPANY

Faster growing than Alcoa, Billiton, Rio Tinto, Anglo American, Newmont Mining and Alcan.

Vitória–Minas Railway/Expansion
Tubaráo Port/Infrastructures
Carajás Mines/Amazon
Compánhia Siderúgica Nacional SA

AFTER 10+ YEARS OF EMPIRE BUILDING

I AM RETURNING TO MY AMERICAN HOME-BASE

GOOD REASONS GALORE

PERMANENT CONTACT
HOLLINGSWORTH FARMS
27 ROAMING COVE TRAIL
SPRINGFIELD, MA 33998
(335) 668-3287
MINEMAN@DIGDOWN.COM

DARIEN HOLLINGSWORTH

MARILYN ELAINE VANETTI

203 METTACA DRIVE EAST
WYMAN, OREGON 97345
CELL 503.882.8894
MARILYN@CRIMEWAVE.NET

CRIMINAL BEHAVIOR SPECIALIST

LAW ENFORCEMENT
FEDERAL/STATE
T-TEAM CERTIFIED
U.S. MARSHALL

FUGITIVES
FOREIGN BOUNTIES
DIPLOMATIC NEGOTIATING

SURVEILLANCE
EASTERN EUROPE
MEXICO MAJOR CITIES
SOUTH AMERICA

There are a lot of really miserable dudes out there. Screwy women too. I can nail them both.

Through NEUTRAL science.

MORE TRUE THAN THE LIARS

503.882.8894
That's the number.

VANETTI
That's the name.

CRIME
That's the GAME.

VLADAMIR STEPAN TROFIMOVITCH

VLADAMIR
STEPAN
TROFIMOVITCH

BUSINESS TURNAROUND SPECIALIST

Track Record Since 1993

Mattal Toys
Yousef & Co.
Bridgestone
Saudi Airway
SEC Trusts
Causa &Roma
Frandco Inc.

I turned these companies and many of their subsidiaries into profit centers by installing rigid IT systems, creating new accounting channels, revamping pricing strategies and implementing "Creative Future Wheel" brainstorming sessions in which employees were encouraged to participate for rewards.

HOTEL MIRAMAR / ISLA MICONDO BEACH

PESTANA EQUADOR ROÇÃ JOÃO RESORT

DEMOCRATIC REPUBLIC OF SÃO TOMÉ É PRÎNCIPE

WEST AFRICA — "CHOCOLATE ISLANDS"

vladdy@sao–tome–choco.com/hotmiramar

Heather Kalinki Chapperwall

SONG WRITER & STAGE DESIGNER

PLAYS & SONGS

"Man's Best Fiend"

"Do Dates"

"Modern Voids"

"The Absent Thee"

"Now In New York?"

"Miss You, Sort Of"

"Cellular Hildegáard"

"A Prince of Errors"

"Walking Deserts"

"Swimming Oceans"

"A Rat Trap Dance"

"My Broken Ballet"

"Warning! It's Me!"

"Total Webness"

"Talkytalk"

238 ELM STREET
NATASHA, NEBRASKA 39912
TELEPHONE 464.288.68432
EMAIL KALINKI@IBEME.NET

Don't leave QC & QA behind.
They may not make it back.

▲▲▲▲▲▲▲▲▲▲▲▲▲▲▲▲▲▲▲▲▲▲▲▲▲▲▲▲▲▲▲▲▲▲

2004–2006
EUROPEAN ORGANISATION FOR ASTRONOMICAL RESEARCH IN THE SOUTHERN HEMISPHERE (CHILE)

DOCUMENTATION DIRECTOR
La Silla Paranal Observatory
Submillimetre Array (Andes)
Frontline Technologies

2000–2004
NORWEGO/COMMERCO NORTH SEA RESEARCH EXPLORATION

DOCUMENT CONTROL MANAGER
Ocean Rig ASA Drilling Vessels
Engineering Progress Reports
Power & OFE/BFE Commissioning
ABB/Hydralift Variation Orders

1996–2000
UNION GLOBITES ENVIRO LLC

CONTROLS DIRECTOR
Global Black Mouse Holes

1991–1996
CHINO SHANGHAI FU CHOW

DC DIRECTOR
Manufacuturing Ecomechanics

A BRIEF OUTLINE
OF
CONTROL MATTERS
DOCUMENTATION DIRECTOR

CRITICAL ISSUES
Construction Status Reports
Structural Integration & Risk Managing

VARIATION ORDERS
Engineering Revisions: Planned/Evolved
Revisions: Safety Concerns & Approvals

PROGRESS REPORTS
Contractual Obligations & Completions
Percentages Month-to-Month
Key Marks & Funding Milestones
Weight Reports & Bare Hulls

MANNING & PERFORMANCE
Engineering & Production Personnel
Instrumentation & Telecommunications

SCHEDULING
Schedules vs. Actuals (Graphs & Charts)

STRUCTURAL
Supplier Documented Material Revs.

DOCUMENT CONTROL DIRECTOR

SIGFRIED MANCHAK

Rigzshaussen No. X–203
Karl–Schwarzchild–Str. 2
D–85748 near Munich
GERMANY
documentman@agency.com
drilloil@deepinthesea.net

Avaña Maria de Gorbari~Estoña

Avenida Presidente Masaryk 360 ✮ Colonia Polanco ✮ 11560 Mexico City
Distrito Federal, Mexico ✮ +52-55-5255-15-52 ✮ gorbari@meximart.net

I'm no WONDER WOMAN, but it's NO WONDER they miss me when I'm gone.

INTERNATIONAL LICENSING

Latin American Markets
Design, Manufacture, Rights & Spin-offs
SINCE 1982 – REGISTERED PRODUCT LINES

Fashion Mavens	Heartstoppers
Marano of Italia	Swissworkshøven
Shoe-In	RollRRock Concerts
Pretty Polly Favors	Movie Stars Clothes
La Dolce Vitamins	KiddmanCole Ltd.
InYourFace Makeup	China Sea Gardens
St. Tropez Beach	Club Gitmo Apparel
Naruto Deko Boko	Ropes & Robes
Glamour Girliemen	Suzy Swims Deep
CirqueMex du Soleil	Moo Goo Clay
Ding Bing Bong	Chesterfield Cos.

I have been a creative innovator in Latin America for over 20 years, saying the right things at the right times to the right people. As proof of my ability to bend minds and turn trends, I have placed licensed brands in places and with people never even considered before me. I have been a knife in the stale waters of product imaging and brand building in a world-class, growing marketplace of young consumers, and I can back up every word I say with facts and point-of-sale examples. Just ask, and I'll tell.

HOTEL MANAGEMENT

26 ISLAND WAY
NAPLES, FL 33223
HOTELIER@GOTOSTAY.COM
917.909.5005 HOME
917.909.3384 CELL
917.999.3320 FAX

Stormy weather doesn't bother me.
I like the excited swell of a crowd.
After all, a hotel is shelter for the soul, too.

Dear Reader,
Here are some of my broiling seas and most memorable voyages.

RITZ-PLAZA ARUBA, 2001 to the present.

I have transformed this battered facility into a first-rate structure with color-ful rooms and expanded suites, adding wrought iron balconies and a luxurious day spa. Reservations: six months deep and occupancy rates could not be better.

HOTEL CARLETON ISLE, 1997 to 2000.

I rebuilt this historical hotel from the bottom up by hiring a new manage-ment staff, who in turn established a brand new service staff whose operation is now in the limelight of the industry.

THE EYE'S INN, 1991 to 1997.

I began as a night auditor and ended at the top managing this flagship chain across the Pacific Basin. Created successful "Ship's Master" gourmet restaurants.

Edward James Hopper

CATHRYNE Li Li YANG

123 SEQUOIA LANE   ALBUQUERQUE, NM 88888 LILI@YANG.COM

❀

DON'T LET SLEEPING DOGS LIE WHEN THEY WAKE THEY BITE

MANAGER OF SHOPPING EXPERIENCE

WHAT DO *YOU* DO WHEN BOTH CHOICES ARE RISKY?

Here's what I do: Make creative decisions that judge the risks in terms of acceptable losses for predictable gains. The market is a chess game and if your intent is to hold onto every pawn, your Queen will die from a lack of oxygen. Marketplace dynamics are benevolently violent and indiscriminating; they don't care which competitors fall by the wayside. Winner takes all. And all it takes is a winner. That's me.

WORCESTER ETAIL STORENETS   2002 TO 2006

VP, Shopping Experience: www and conversion of 200+ US stores; 2,300 employees; 16 US/Irish call centers; 4 DP centroplexes; Top 10 Sales.

WESTERN GULF SHORES NATIONAL OUTLETS   1999 TO 2002

Manager, Shopping Experience: www and 114+ US/Mexican stores; 800 employees; 3 Indian call centers; Top 25 "Fast Company" Sales 02.

HALFADOLLAR "CHEAP-O" DISCOUNTS   1990 TO 1997

Shopping Experience Innovator: company's entry into electronic sales.

IS IT ME OR IS SUCCESS GETTING A BAD RAP?

SPOT MARKET MANAGER

Cathay Holding Company
GuruOil Netco Corporation
SemboCorp Marine PLC
Daewoo Japan Companies
Symbol Technologies Inc.
El Paso Guidant Corp.
Statoll Bertelsmann ASA
OAO Ruskinsky & Kleinin
Playtex Visteon AG
Mizuho-TowerStream Ltd.
Havas Heekin Exploration

THE MARKET MANAGER

Bluto may not be tough enough for this business because it is tough with a capital "T" and it starts on the other side of the world about the same time you're going to sleep and you may wake up to a nightmare of raging refinery fires, tanker collisions and aging, monolithic Iranian clerics working with OPEC sheiks. All in a day's work for me.

OLLI PEKKA KALZO

HINDUSTAN PETROLEUM CORPORATION LIMITED/MDPL TERMINALS PROJECT
Corrigendum No. 2, DGM (Contracts), Mecon Limited, Bangalore, India
+91-80-2657 1661 to 1668   olli-pekka@hindustan-dotin.com

WHO'S REALLY SAFE?

CHRONOLOGICAL TRACK RECORD

Pre- and Post-WWW

I worked my way up the ranks of Gladstone Cooper International as their #1 Documentation/Information Control Supervisor. When we were acquired by Tasakoski Corporation in 1999, I was promoted to Web Developer & Director of New Business Prospects for US & Europe.

In 2002, with VisionSpace Industries ASA, I was the one who introduced net-storage servers to Belgium financial companies.

Check out the mags for my articles and reviews by my peers, if you will, please.

Bachelor's of Fine Arts
University of Amsterdam

DATA STORAGE

FTP SPECIALIST

OLD STUFF IN NEW PLACES

BUTTONED DOWN TIGHT

I keep things in their place.

My record is as good as gold.

Safe, secure, systematized.

Ankeliki Sonalan

Dashka Polanka No. 4 Lake Seliger/Moscow 5A-1k ankeliki@datahrush.net

SAUD AL-FAISAL ABDULLAH MITAB

House of Sand Tower No. 3
1 Royal Payne – ARSE Plaza
Lorrytowne, Scotland 3A9 B2X

mitab-be-king@sandhouse.com

Deals Made, No Blinking

Camel Trading to Containerships

Since the 80s I have been involved as the 'agent provacateur' in shaking up major companies stumbling in the global marketplace. You may have heard of me, maybe not, but be sure that I know this tricky business of international trade, from discounted customs stamps at cheap portside facilities to EU tariffs and duties at major western destinations. Here is a quick list of some of my customers and contacts in the industry.

DUBAI / SHANGHAI / NEW YORK / DUSSELDORF / KUALA LUMPUR

SKY FU-LEE   EVANGELOS SHIPPING   PISTIOLIS & STAVROS

RAILWAY ZHLUDNEV   DATASPHERE INTERNATIONAL

DE-WAAL CONVERS   CHINA SEAS NURAPASHI   GOMEZ TRADING

STANISLAV VALDIKAVKAZ COS.   TEKI-KALOYEROS CORP.

MONKA WEED   HUDSON CITY SEA-CORP.   NUTRINOSYSTEMS

THOMAS WEASEL PARTNERS   ATLAS CRANE COMPANY

ALLION   PIPER JAFFRAY   PACIFIC CREST

BOENING & SCATTERGOOD   QUOSIMO   LEG MASON

PORTEGE   LIBRETTO   ZEITGEIST SUPERCELL

CSABA CSERE   KHALIDI NOTYET

Marcia Anne Turkenov

1600 WELLINGTON BOULEVARD
CHICAGO, ILLINOIS 22998

TELEPHONE 298–337–4028 #28
CELLULAR 298–448–6630

GO AHEAD!

HOG THE MARKET!

THAT'S WHAT I LIKE TO DO.

marciaknows@gonehogwild.com

I have been a creative force behind product placement and highly innovative marketing programs that are linked to major national brands. My career has led me from the ranks as an original product packager and pork bellies market analyst to advertising and promotions (coupons) manager, to eventual director of corporate marketing strategies and offshoring manufacture planning. Balancing cost reductions without undue risks (labor shortfalls, product inventories, JIT gaps) and margin improvements (from 1.8% to 39% in last five years) is my forté. I know the packaged meat business as well as anyone working. I have both formal academic credentials and vast practical knowledge in this highly competitive industry.

PRABHAKAR RAGHAVAN

CHIEF TECHNOLOGY OFFICER
EXPERT ALGORITHMIST
MASTER DIALECTICIST

3233 CHEYENNE HEAD HILLS

GREAT DEEP CANYON, IDAHO 39221

213.297.7883 OR 213.999.3567

luckylingo@dogma.com

Blackboard Message #1

OUTER SPACE! INNER SPACE!

<u>What's</u> the difference?

NUMBERS = NUMBERS

OFTEN MIND-NUMBING

<u>BUT</u>

NEVER TO ME!

Blackboard Message #2

MARKET SHARE! PERCENTAGES!

<u>There's</u> a lot of differences!

NUMBERS ≈ NUMBERS

VERY MIND-BLINDING

<u>BUT</u>

NOT TO ME!

BUILDING AN INTELLIGENT & LOGICAL NANOTECHNOLOGY

from the inside out is not something you want to play with if you have an aversion to failure. It hurts. The brick walls never stop. You live with them. At least, I do. And then once in a thousand tries a crack opens up and the next thing you know you are leading the whole team into a new dimension of possibilities you were afraid to even think of as practical before. That's the thrill of leadership. It's more than a duty. It's a passion.

BELINDA STAAR

LET'S FACE IT.
THE WORLD'S A MESS.
IT'S TIME TO GET YOUR ACT
TOGETHER. FOR THAT, YOU
COULD USE MY TALENT.
TRUST ME. TALK TO ME.
888-IAM-FAST. 24/7
ASK FOR BELINDA.

KARL VAN RUE

READY FOR HIRE RIGHT NOW

Auto Master Vintage Vendor

VAN RUE FAMILY HOUSE
ONE RIVERVIEW CIRCLE
401 WEST MAIN STREET
LOUISVILLE, KY 40202
502.568.2100
AUTOAUCTIONEERS.COM

MY BEST SALES MANY YEARS

1929 Duesenberg J-249
Murphy Torpedo Roadster

1961 Mercedes-Benz
300D Cabriolet

1934 V-12 Pierce Arrow

1951 Talbot Lago T26

1929 Ford Model A Woody

1931 Minerva Rollston

1953 Cadillac Ghia

1969 Lincoln
Continental Mark IV

1928 Isotta Fraschini Baron

1960 Austin Healey 3000
MK 1 BT7

1959 Mercedes-Benz
190SL Roadster

1948 Tucker Sedan

1939 Alpha Romeo
6C 2500 Sport

Marie Selena St. Thomas

CHEF SUPERIORE

242 Fifth Street ❧ Sleeping Dog, Kansas 66206 ❧ 913-555-0288

When I cook & serve, *my plate* is full. And so is the RESTAURANT.

MY MENU

Supervising Chef at BORDEAUX STEAK HOUSE in Kansas City for 6 years. Restaurant sales increased 140% during my tenure, and profits averaged an increase of 18% annually. Five-star classed in all lists (2001 to 2006).

Supervising Chef/Sommelier at THE BAY in San Francisco for 5 years. Restaurant sales increased 122% in last year alone (2000) and close to that for all years prior, as well as major facility expansion and specialty dining rooms which I managed for pricey catering events to Californian high rollers and Asian partners.

Before that, typical restaurant apprenticeships and certifications, from Manhattan to Rome, including working with *Pablo Renoir* in Paris for ten months.

I MAKE
REAL ESTATE DEALS
REALLY HAPPEN

1980 TO NOW

Pointe Timeless
Lake Hideaway
Legends at Chateau
Ladder Canyon Ranch
Litchfield Bridges
Dutchess Estates
Berkshire Mountain
Big Sky Springs
Horseshoe Bay
The Bristol
Teton Blue Valley
Biltmore Forest
Bald Headed Island
The Tesoro Trillium
Yellowstone Club
Canary Station
3 Creeks Ranch

plus
CityScraperPlazas

mark rothko

510 TENNYSON AVENUE
NASHVILLE, TN 39222
(502) 438-9929

IN THIS **ROUGH & TUMBLE** business you can easily **LOSE** YOUR SHIRT if you're not really careful.

make-it-mark@reallocation.com

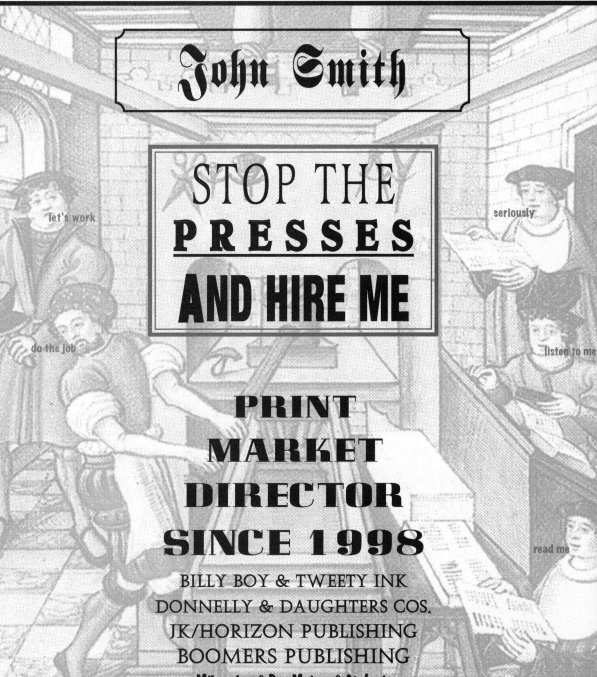

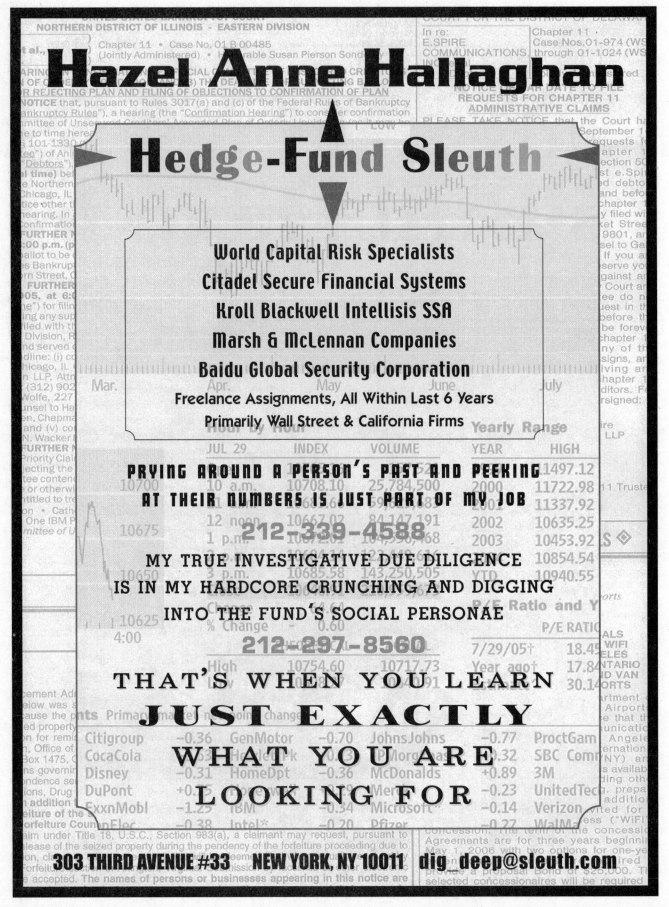

JUMP ON A PLANE AND FLY WITH ME

ROBERTO OCALA–JONES

3300 Calle Sangria/No. 3
Montes Apalaches, Guadalajara
800.339.5839
extours@flywithme.com.mx

MEX–XEMPT VACATIONPRO® SEMINARS
PROMOTIONS & COMPANY DIRECTOR

2004 to Present

I am the man who made this company happen in a big way. MEX-EXEMPT TOURS & SEMINARS was the first NAFTA-oriented vacation package offering tax-deductible workshops in Mexican resort facilities. Since I took over U.S. and European marketing and promotions, sales have spiked considerably despite increasing airfare costs due to inflated oil prices. This enterprise, backed by Salt Lake City Venture Capital, has been so successful we are drafting plans for Belize-Exempt and Costa Rica-Exempt programs. We currently have in place the following VacationPro® Seminars:

ACAPULCO	AGUASCALIENTES	CAULIACAN	CHIUAHUA
Tax Law Sunsets	*Engineering Cityscapes*	*Selling Dreams*	*PR Disaster Planning*
Banking & Parole	*Autonomous Infrastructure*	*Market Packaging*	*PR Recoveries*
COATZACOALCOS	DURANGO	GUANAJUATO	HERMOSILLO
Publishing Technology	*Pharmaceutical Brands*	*R.E. & Death*	*Manufacturing Metals*
Paper Technologies	*FDA & Patent Issues*	*Unreal Estates*	*Plant Management Risk*
LA PAZ	NUEVO LAREDO	MAZATLAN	MERIDA
Insuring Terrorism	*Red Light Districts*	*Computer Hardware*	*Software Platforms*
Reinsuring Hedging	*Boys Town Surveys*	*Memory & Drives*	*Crossover IT Systems*
OBREGON	QUERETARO	TOLUCA	ZACATECAS
Hedge Funds Today	*The Autobus Industry*	*Distribution Design*	*Prison Industries*
Protecting Fortunes	*Truck Electronics*	*Conveying Systems*	*Materials Strength*

Bachelor of Business Administration
University of Texas b001

AVAILABLE FOR INTERVIEWS NOW

REFERENCES UPON REQUEST

WILL RELOCATE ANYWHERE SOUTH

SAMPLE BIOBLOG #53

Lilliana Belina Muzkow

Street "Llir Konushevci" No. 8   Prishtinë/Pristina, Kosovo   Tel. +381 38 500 400

lmuso@kta-kosovo.org or showme@euromix.net.kv

AUDIO VISUAL
Events Manager

VENTURE CAPITAL PROGRAMS
KOSOVO TRUST AGENCY

Since 2000, I have been critically instrumental in the official formulation and bidding process for the following major Kosovian infrastructure and private enterprise projects totalling in the hundreds of millions of dollars known as THE SIXTH WAVE.

Bottling Plant Suhareke Brewery & Bottling Plant	$42M	$12M	**Produkt Mitröviça** Agricultural Farm Land
Teka Commerce Trading Index Facility	$9M	$16M	**Stacioni Bujquesore** Agriculture (Chicken Farms)
Kosovarja Kalpaseen Bread & Packaging Factories	$22M	$18M	**EuroMetalKV** Metal Processing
Lavertari Moltov Dairy Farms & Distribution	$19M	$38M	**Pashtriku** Hotels & Restaurants
Trasing & Goldwell Road & Bridge Construction	$220M	$16M	**Mirusha** Construction Materials
Vinex Mining Corp. Metal Processing	$38M	$49M	**KHT "Kosova" (Sloga)** Water Systems

I know how to make a BIG DEAL out of a BIG DEAL.

In Kazakhstan or Kalishnikov or Kansas City.

In person, on screen, in print.

Michael Bineto Zepatone

2059 Mason
Burlingtown
Georgia 39982
(355) 668-2243

DEATH SPECIALIST
Funerals & Wakes
Wills & Gatherings
Transnational Situations

Messages
(355) 668-8713
E-Mail
zep@Udie.org

18 YEARS *IN THIS* INDUSTRY. A **LEADER** IN Today's Trends & FUTURE NEEDS. *I KNOW* **THIS BIZ** *WELL.*

We *could* talk About Death and dying 'till the cows come home, but you get right down to it, only EXPERIENCE helps.

CORPORATE COMMERCIAL FINANCIAL
NATIONAL NETWORKS DIRECTOR
SUPPLY CHAIN & CHANNEL DISTRIBUTION
PRICING & MARKETING MANAAGER

WENDELLA MOYE

NUMBERS MANAGER
SALES MANAGER
ACCOUNT MANAGER

COMMINIQUES
MAILDIRECT

#4-UZ PRAGUE PLAZA № 016
HAPSBERGEN DEN. 0B97M-E335
Telefon 01.100.933.229
windy_wendy@sellersalt.biz

In our competitive and often uncivil sales and marketing business, Ms. Moye is called the *windy mistress of change* because she is ever on the prowl for new trends to seal her deals. She would be a great 3-card monte street artist who would take your money. – *A Client*

NUMBERS DON'T LIE & PRETTY PICTURES
DON'T TELL *THE WHOLE STORY*

BUT THEY GIVE A PRETTY GOOD IDEA OF MY DAY

37 FIELD OFFICES & 16-STATE REGION

 46+ Sales Teams **WITH A 86%** Conversion Rate

$835,000 p.a. Team Average

$10,000 **BONUS 3 YEARS STRAIGHT (04, 05, 06)**

I have a theory: A sales cycle has its own rhythm and you cannot force it into an unnatural direction. Tuning into your customer's particular future is the only workable process for discovering their specific buy-cycles; and matching these item for item with a cunning strategy that provides for their needs and wants—at the most appropriate time—is the absolute key to closing.

It's hard work, but nothing else works!

VINNIE CHANG

A NEW HAND AT OLD TRICKS IN THE BUSINESS OF DESIGNING OFFICE SYSTEMS

I AM PERSISTENT

I AM DETERMINED

I AM IMAGINATIVE

I AM RESOURCEFUL

I AM GROUNDED

I AM POSITIVE

I AM VIGOROUS

I AM SHARING

I AM GROUNDED

Y E A R S

2005–2006
DATACORP BLDG.
IBM WEB OFFICE
NETWORLD LTD.
2004–2005
BIG DADDY LEGS
OFFICECOOP INC.
SAMMIES NATIONWIDE
2003–2004
WELLS FARGO
NAN CHOW CO.

I AM POSITIVE

Y E A R S

2002–2003
EXPOENTIAL ENTER.
GOOGLEBLOT INC.
TRUMP YOU TOO CO.
2001–2002
MONA LISA LISTCO.
KOREAN SINGSONG
DOT INDIAN COS.
2000–2001
UMAMBO

I AM VIGOROUS

Y E A R S

1999–2000
RED RYDER STORAGE
HOLLYWOOD MAVENS
THE YOUTH FACTORY
ALFIE'S ALZIES INC.
REGISTERED LOONIES
1997–1999
WARHOLDOFF INC.
BAZOOKAS UNLIMITED
THIRD WORLD RETAIL
SAUDIS

I AM SHARING

Y E A R S

1995–1997
EAST CHINA TRADING
LOWER PRICES INC.
BARGAIN HUNTER INC.
CLOSE-OUTS CO.

Before That
DUFFELDORF & DODO
MACHINE GUN BLUES
NETWORK REALTIME CO.
PENNSYLVANIA DUTCHCO

I AM BALANCED

I AM HONORABLE

I AM ENERGIZED

I AM POISED

AWARDS

"Best Office Design"
2005
NY Design Group

Top Creative Designer
O'Malley 2003

The Bloodwork Award
2000
Nights National

BIOBLOG

U.S. PASSPORT

FREELANCE U.S.A.

CONTRACT ASIA

FIRST CLASS REFS

SOLID PORTFOLIO

AVAILABLE NOW

BIOBLOG

CHINESE-AMERICAN

FLUENT MANDARIN

WIDELY TRAVELLED

COMPUTER SAVVY

CHICAGO INSTITUTE
OF ART MFA, BFA
MARRIED

AWARDS

"Office Innovator"
2004
NY-NJ Pro/Design

1st Place/Designlines
Maverick Award 1999

Honorable Mention
1997 & 2002
Architectural Digest

StudioPlace 4   East Riverwalk   New York, NY 10003
chinang@verizon.net   cell 212.212.2121

Merilee Wellweather

| 9000 Canyon Road | Phoenix, Arizona 68425 | Telephone 444.323.8892 | belo@bluesky.net |
| Forsythe Court 835 | 309 The Hedgerow W5A | Leeds L51 5JW England | 0870 240 3087 |

(POS)

POINT-OF-SALE is MY SPECIALTY

POS PLACEMENT STRATEGIES – POS PACKAGING & BRANDING

POS BREAKAWAYS & COUPONS – POS PRODUCT LINKING

POS BARCODE TECHNOLOGIES – POS MULTIMARKET TIERS

My History & International Marketing Management

A Record of Creative & Innovative Marketing Strategies

Edinburgh Learning Technologies Limited: *2005 to Present*

The Royal Bank of Scotland Group: *2003 to 2005*

Aston Martin Luxury Automobiles: *2004*

Instituto de Empressa Business Programs: *2001 to 2003*

Liverpool Worldwide Labour Poole: *2000 to 2001*

Katholicke Universiteit Leuven Programmes: *1998 to 2000*

Amsterdam Windows Corporation: *1993 to 1998*

Ghent Ghetto Global Companies: *1990 to 1993*

My Formal Studies & Special Training in Marketing

MBA TIME – 2000

[TECHNOLOGIES & INNOVATIVE MANAGEMENT & ENTREPRENEURSHIP]

Ecole nationale des ponts et chaussees & Institut de Francáis (Paris)

The Autonomous Management School of Ghent University (1988)

Kohlo Friedan Institute of Business Management (1992)

Besoldungsgruppe Amt für Zusammenarbeit (2000)

If you are not sure if you are coming or going, and if the competition is sniping at your ankles and you keep running out of petrol at the wrong time, I can help you escape. I can turbocharge your POS via integration and innovation, streaming and streamlining, and a steady hand.

LORD LEE OXBURGH

SHINNECOCK INDIAN RESERVATION

Tonytown Villas MA3   Soppyville, West Virginia 39900   (335) 553-0998   oxman@lordlyife.net

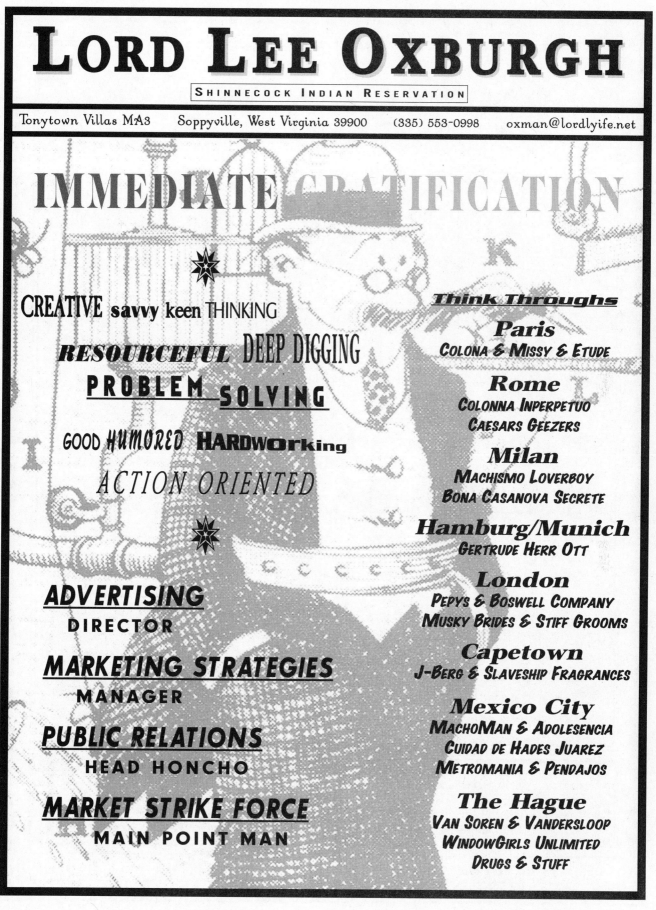

IMMEDIATE GRATIFICATION

CREATIVE savvy keen THINKING

RESOURCEFUL DEEP DIGGING

PROBLEM SOLVING

GOOD HUMORED HARDWOrking

ACTION ORIENTED

ADVERTISING
DIRECTOR

MARKETING STRATEGIES
MANAGER

PUBLIC RELATIONS
HEAD HONCHO

MARKET STRIKE FORCE
MAIN POINT MAN

Think Throughs

Paris
COLONA & MISSY & ETUDE

Rome
COLONNA INPERPETUO
CAESARS GEEZERS

Milan
MACHISMO LOVERBOY
BONA CASANOVA SECRETE

Hamburg/Munich
GERTRUDE HERR OTT

London
PEPYS & BOSWELL COMPANY
MUSKY BRIDES & STIFF GROOMS

Capetown
J-BERG & SLAVESHIP FRAGRANCES

Mexico City
MACHOMAN & ADOLESENCIA
CUIDAD DE HADES JUAREZ
METROMANIA & PENDAJOS

The Hague
VAN SOREN & VANDERSLOOP
WINDOWGIRLS UNLIMITED
DRUGS & STUFF

IT IS TIME

TO GET A GRIP ON COSTS

KEELA CAN UNTIE THE KNOTS

SHE CAN PLUG THE HOLES & STOP THE BLEEDING

SHE understands the cost of TIME and the time LOST MONEY ends up costing.

KEELA BAKNEVSKY

As Controller & Treasurer, I have a strong ability to analyze financials and all aspects of a company's operations to ascertain real vs. intangible costs, and to determine where hidden costs can be revealed. My personality is no-nonsense and practical-oriented; I am demanding but rely more on my own instincts than I do on the reports from others, which are often inaccurate or omit the most critical data, accidentally or purposely. I have adapted a policy of all costs are flexible and coordinate and control numerical flow, such as from balance sheets and subsidiary P&L statements, to one inclusive result: What's missing? And why? From my personal experience as an accountant and CPA, I don't have a distrust of people in general, but I believe people have little understanding of numbers.

WORK		
2005 –	Global Corps Sales/Services LLC
2002–05	Shell Oil Offshore Groups PLC
2000–02	Kosovo Trust Agency/Pashtriku
1995–00	Israeli Ministry of Industry & Trade
1992–95	The Control Risks Group SSA

SCHOOL		
2005	"British Tax Law" Old Parliament School
2002	"Offshore Shelters" & "Limited Risks"
2000	CPA, The International School of London
1999	"Foreign Capital Exchange" (I & III & V)
1997	MBA in Finance, Wharton School

SUITE 1505M · 96 ALBION PLAZA ◆ 77 GRANVILLE ROAD, T.S.T. ◆ KOWLOON, HONG KONG ◆ (852) 2794·1328

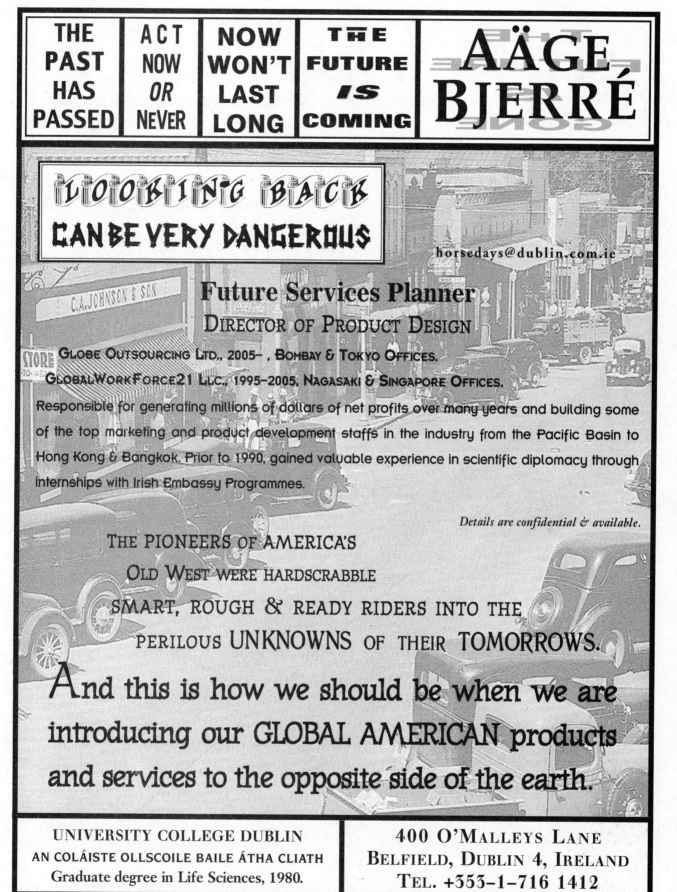

| THE PAST HAS PASSED | ACT NOW OR NEVER | NOW WON'T LAST LONG | THE FUTURE IS COMING | AÄGE BJERRÉ |

LOOKING BACK CAN BE VERY DANGEROUS

horsedays@dublin.com.ie

Future Services Planner
DIRECTOR OF PRODUCT DESIGN

GLOBE OUTSOURCING LTD., 2005– , BOMBAY & TOKYO OFFICES.
GLOBALWORKFORCE21 LLC., 1995–2005, NAGASAKI & SINGAPORE OFFICES.
Responsible for generating millions of dollars of net profits over many years and building some of the top marketing and product development staffs in the industry from the Pacific Basin to Hong Kong & Bangkok. Prior to 1990, gained valuable experience in scientific diplomacy through internships with Irish Embassy Programmes.

Details are confidential & available.

THE PIONEERS OF AMERICA'S
OLD WEST WERE HARDSCRABBLE
SMART, ROUGH & READY RIDERS INTO THE
PERILOUS UNKNOWNS OF THEIR TOMORROWS.

And this is how we should be when we are introducing our GLOBAL AMERICAN products and services to the opposite side of the earth.

UNIVERSITY COLLEGE DUBLIN	400 O'MALLEYS LANE
AN COLÁISTE OLLSCOILE BAILE ÁTHA CLIATH	BELFIELD, DUBLIN 4, IRELAND
Graduate degree in Life Sciences, 1980.	TEL. +353–1–716 1412

350 Oak Tree Lane
Johnson City, TN 88332
(309) 992-4458

Sara Robinson

fisherwoman.com
(888) FOR–FISH
fishtrain@lake.com

FISHING
is about planning & analyzing
and so is
Business

THEY CALL IT telemarketing BUT IT'S REALLY TELLING MARKETING.

NOT ONLY THAT, MOST MANAGERS FIND IT HARD TO TELL WHAT WORKS AND WHAT DOESN'T.

NOT ME

BECAUSE THERE'S **BAIT**, AND THEN THERE'S BAIT

AND YOU HAVE TO KNOW HOW TO WIGGLE THE WORM

EXPERT TM MANAGER

Team Leader from the Floor

M.A. Human Services 1993
Vanderbilt University
SALES & MARKETING SEMINARS
Offshore Experience
Confidential Portfolio Available

CAREER TRACKING

2005 to Present
A Major Credit Card Issuer
TM TROUBLESHOOTING:
INDIA & NORTH ENGLAND

1999 to 2005
Land & Land/Kodak International
RESOURCE DIRECTOR
Call Center Services

HWANG WOO SUK
PROCESS MANAGER

92 UMKHANYAKUDE PLAZA
DISTRICT OF CHUNGCHEONG   SOUTH KOREA
tel +44 (0)1707 259 383
autosukwoo@mobilegolulu.net

My love of automobiles and other wheeled machines goes back to my bike riding days in Chungcheon, when I often travelled with my family to Seoul to see movies and watch the busy streets. My resourceful nature led me to invent my own auto-car from abandoned washing machine parts and farming implements. I was so taken by these machines that I raced them against local scooters, often crashing them on the rocky roads that passed for highways. My training in Detroit and at The College for Creative Studies taught me drafting design and IT management programs, but it has been my heartfelt compulsion to drive that has keep me going, looking for the perfect design.

AUTO DESIGN & PROCESS MASTER

Areas of Expertise Worldwide

Powertrain Road Mapping

International Strategies for Hybrid Cars

Advancing Safety Technologies

Models Under Globalization

Global Branding & Design

Japan's Luxury Car Market

New Process Technologies

Soaring Material Prices

Automotive Society Brandbandization

Automotive Design in Guangzhou

Reducing Development Time & IT

Blue Chip Auto Parts Makers

Chinese Competitive Manufacturing

Automotive Software Design

COMPANIES & CLIENTS

Design Manager/Process Consultant

Period of 2003 to current design work:

NISSAN EUROPE OPERATIONS
Phaedra SUV, OEDIPUS SERIES
Mex-a-Tex Series, OAXACAN
DriveOver Sports Coupe, HEMISPHERIC

DEUTSCHAUSENHOFFER LTD.
DREAMCOUPE ® Convertible
MACHINE-LINE LOCOCYCLE ®
MOTO GOZO II ®

Period of 1985 to about 2003:

BENTLEY BRITISH MOTOR CO.
Lady Di, LUXURY SPORTS-SUV

RUSKYKONOV–FIAT LTD.
FIAT: Realto & Finito
RUSKYKONOV/CZECK: 'The Rolly' & Blotto
CZECK: Cabbo & Warbly
Under Contract: Rusko Roulette

SAMPLE BIOBLOG #63

Neikko Nagamine

BIOMETRIC IDENTIFIER SPECIALIST

neikko-knows@secure-biojap.org

A tried and true professional since 1994:

- Mitsubishi Tokyo Financial Group
- Fujitsuko Ltd. & Mizuhlco Bank Ltd.
- Sumitomo Financial Group
- Hitachi Ltd. THROUGH THE M&A OF SELECTCOM LLC
- Akira Wakabayashi Consulting

I have been personally very instrumental in developing PalmHandScan® technologies utilized in Japan's expanding mobile cellphone and cash card businesses. This extraordinary new verification technology is based on biometrics that are conducive to secure imaging services, and it is now estimated that NTT DoCoMo will employ some 8m of these PHS-Z cards by 2010. According to "Sun Today" (Shinji Munekuni), this is the "oncoming crest of future electronic financial transactions security." As Product Team Creative Director and Innovation Managing Leader, I have forged important alliances in all the related supplier chains and manufacturing industries.

I know this business like the back of my hand.

KATSUAKI WATANABE

c/o ISLAMIC DEVELOPMENT BANK
POB 5925, Jeddah 21432
Kingdom of Saudi Arabia
Fax +966 2 6372069
katsuwa@isdb.org

CORPORATE OFFICE PARK
CONSTRUCTION MANAGER

IT'S A DIFFERENT WORLD THESE DAYS.
THAT'S WHY I SPECIALIZE IN HIGH
SECURITY FORTIFIED BUILDINGS.

IT'S WHAT I DO **&** WHAT WE NEED

Since 2000
SECURE GLOBAL PROPERTIES
SENSITIVE COMPARTMENTED
INFORMATION FACILITIES
BOMBPROOF BLACK BOX BUILDINGS
INVISIBLE FENCES & INTELLIGENT ACCESS
CLOSED COAT ANTI-MICROWAVE WINDOWS
LOCKWRAP® TECHNOLOGIES
LUCENTLIGHT STRUCTURAL CODE

A Partial List of Clients

Booz Allen Hamilton	WW3 Technology Inc.
GreatBrit BattleCom	Hummer Transport
Northwrap Grooman	Lockheed Hellfire Cos.
Titan War Corporation	Islamo Trapco Inc.
Marine Landing Science	IBMM Integrated
London Bombs Fallco.	Great Guns & Rifles

ROMANO POLYNSKA

Petroleum Fire Manager

WHEN & WHERE

2006–OAO NOVATEK
2006–OAO GAZPROM
2005–OAO XONOTEC
2005–SAUDI PERMENIAN
2005–BP/PETROCHINA
2004–BP/SAUDI LLC
2004–LUKOIL
2004–MEXI-PETROFINA
2003–CHINA DRILLING
2003–BRAZILIAN ORE
2002–PETROFALLEN
2002–LG PHILLIPS AG
2001–ARAMACO
1999–GENI-CHEVRON
1998–ROYAL DUTCH
1996–SHELL NORSEA

309 NO. 21 RUE DEPRÍES
LENINGRADSKI, RUSSIA
romanoamano@poly.net

Rachel Worthington

Technology Director & Creative Manager

IMPLEMENTATION MANAGER: CONCEPTS & STRATEGY

INFORMATION AND KNOWLEDGE PLANS/DATA SECURITY TRANSITIONS
BUSINESS LANDSCAPE PLANNER, ELECTRONIC ARTS

EXPLORE ME.

I KNOW WHAT I'M DOING & I CAN USE WHAT I KNOW, QUITE WELL.

TECHNOLOGY IS THE MOST CREATIVE USE OF AVAILABLE TIME.

KNOWLEDGE IS THE KEY TO GOOD TIMING, WHICH IS EVERYTHING.

My professional background is as complex and storied as most other tremendously successful people in the top of their field. Like many others, I began in a totally unrelated industry and ended up in "Knowledge Technology" out of curiosity rather than design. As such, my probing into the machinations of VC startups brought me face to face with some one of the brightest and most brash young talents captivated by a company's fancy titles and humongous salaries. Taming these wildchilds into productive children and then into teammates was a task, which proved not only fun but incredibly profitable, as we all ended up making a lot of money. Like most of them, there's more to me than dollars. I want to lead the pack at the crest of the wave. Call on me to see why.

Post Office Box 2994   Harelde Caverne, Australia 34A98E   rachelw@techycrat.org.au

MARK JONES
CREATIVE DESTRUCTOR
GETS THE JOB DONE

FOR EXAMPLE

BUILT LUXURY HOTEL IN TOUGH UPPER END MARKET

REVIVED A FAILING SOUTH AMERICAN AIRLINE

RELOCATED SIXTEEN CHINA FACTORIES TO EUROPE

PUT TOGETHER A DEAL FOR CONTAINERSHIP SHARES

TURNED SLIPPING E-NET BUSINESS INTO MAJOR WINNER

AND THERE'S YET MORE!

Realized a 22% gain in market share in underplayed South American short-flight schedules; reduced shipping costs by implanting supplier chains; expanded delivery distribution systems by bar-coded call-ups; poked holes in luxury market with new service structure aimed at trustfund babies.

"CONTACT ME AT" NUMBERS

(212) 887-3299 OR (338) 228-8511 OR MARKTURNAROUND@WORLDNET.NET

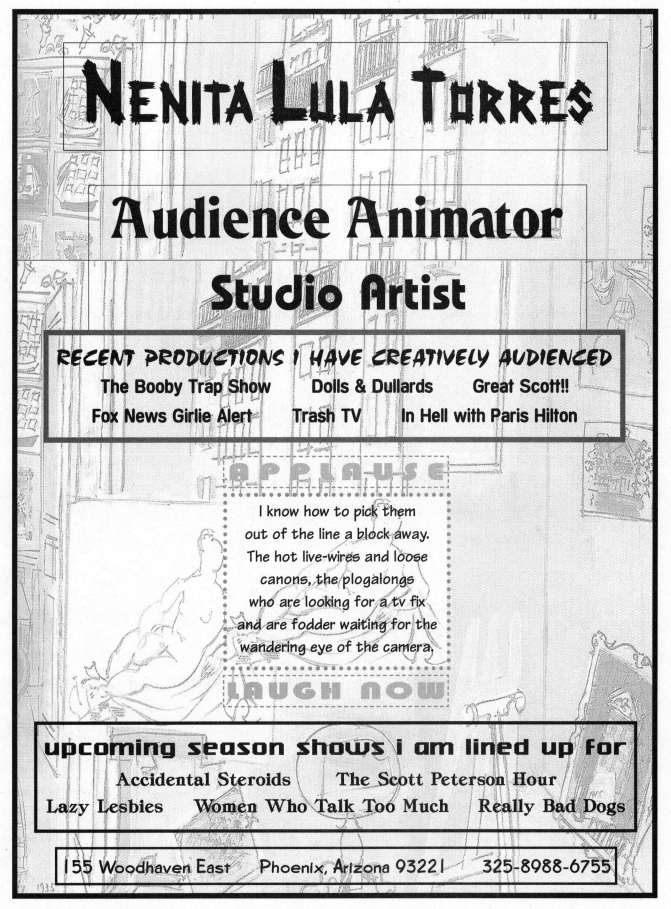

NENITA LULA TORRES

Audience Animator

Studio Artist

RECENT PRODUCTIONS I HAVE CREATIVELY AUDIENCED

The Booby Trap Show   Dolls & Dullards   Great Scott!!

Fox News Girlie Alert   Trash TV   In Hell with Paris Hilton

APPLAUSE

I know how to pick them
out of the line a block away.
The hot live-wires and loose
canons, the plogalongs
who are looking for a tv fix
and are fodder waiting for the
wandering eye of the camera.

LAUGH NOW

upcoming season shows i am lined up for

Accidental Steroids   The Scott Peterson Hour

Lazy Lesbies   Women Who Talk Too Much   Really Bad Dogs

155 Woodhaven East   Phoenix, Arizona 93221   325-8988-6755

WILSON MASINGALE

OPERATIONS CONTROL

RIGID FINANCIAL CONTROLS

Controlling Corporate Problems

a complete & total control freak

MANAGER OF CHANGE
U.S. MARKET TRANSITION

KIKKOMAN JAPAN INC.

A 300-year-ld company.

Report directly to Yuzaburo Mogi, Chairman & CEO, Japan HQ.

Instrumental since 2001 in expanding Kikkoman's U.S. market shares by 10% p.a. as well as an aggressive entrance into the U.S. soymilk market. Negotiated transitional operations in recent joint venture (and planned acquisition of) *Consaktu Industries*, maker of **RuralLiving Vitamins** and other health foods and supplements. Expanded distribution channels beyond supermarkets and developed implementation plan for marketing expansion in Australia. Spearheaded U.S. product r&d for *tsuyu*, *tare* and *shoku-iku*. Helped company reduce European costs by 12.5% in past 14 months by converting customs taxable inventories to Euros.

Before Kikkoman, I was responsible for creating innovative products and adding value to existing brands at several well-known companies. Between them and when I received my graduate degree from Northwestern, I wandered around the world taking a look at what's out there to see. Glad I did, too.

355 Westlake   Sanjo, CA 23992   468.392.5587   talktome@money.net

TIMES HAVE CHANGED & IT'S A DIFFERENT WORLD

SOME THINGS NEVER CHANGE: STRONG LEADERS

JUST ANOTHER DAY OF TOIL AT THE OFFICE
SIFTING THROUGH GRANULES OF DATA
AND GRAINS OF MEANINGFUL CONTENT.

Farming Frameworks

I PLOW

FERTILE FIELDS FOR RAW INFORMATION

TO REAP AND SOW THE HIGHEST YIELDS

3002 Ant Farm Road / Moss Point, MS 39563 / 228.766.3399

seedmanworks@farmland.com or ADM @ 800-FARMMAN

FRANCIS WALSWARK
AGRONOMIST

CREDENTIALS TO DATE

Master of Agricultural Science, Texas A&M University, 1970.

Graduate, Federal Farm Research & Land Studies Program, 1978.

Graduate, Ohio University "Seed Science" Field Program, 1983.

Graduate, Washington University "Farming Genetics" Program, 1988.

Graduate, St. Louis Farmland Center "Lost Seeds" Program, 1992.

Ph.D., Genetic Agronomy, Case Western Reserve, 2000.

Senior Seed Scientist, Archer-Daniel-Midland, 2000 to present.

Seed & Implement Innovator, ADM & Kellog, 1989 to 1992 & 1996 to 1998.

Farm Matrix Planner (Seeding Consultant), 1988 to 1996.

I also grew up on a farm in Nebraska and have a patent on soybean genetics.

MABAK DAE QUEDO

A CAN DO GUY

WORKWORLD

1995–PRESENT
John Wiley & Sons
BEIJING & TOKYO

Founded in 1807, JWS is a global publisher of print and electronic products, specializing in financial, scientific, technical and medical (FSTM) books and journals, professional and consumer books and subscription services; and textbooks and other educational materials for undergraduate and graduate students as well as lifelong learners. JWS provides 'must-have' content to targeted communities of interest. Approximately 25% of global revenue is currently Web-enabled, and is expected to increase to about 40% in 3–5 years.

Publisher & Editorial Director
FSTM CHINA (2004–Present)

Editor & Managing List Director
FSTM JAPAN (2000–2004)

Operations & Management
LONDON/LANCASTERSHIRE & ZURICH & BERN (1990–2000)

MAILING ADDRESS IN THE EAST

2 CLEMENTI LOOP CIRCLE No. 9

SINGAPORE 129809 SINGAPORE

DAEQUEDO@WILEYASIA.COM.SG

FINANCIAL PUBLISHING

Curriculum Vitae

MSc Public Policy & Management 1993
The University of London
Centre for Financial & Management Studies

Financial Restructuring
Acquisition Finance Methods
Asset-Backed Securities
Building Financial Confidence
Crossing Commercial Borders

AMSTERDAM INSTITUTE OF FINANCE
ZURICH UNIVERSITY OF APPLIED SCIENCES
SOLVAY BUSINESS SCHOOL (BELGIUM)

BSc Finance & Accounting 1987
The University of Virginia (USA)

MOST RECENT PUBLICATIONS
Financial Engineering & Econometrics
Global Behavioral Financial Strategies
EU Exchange–Rate Budgeting & Economics
Integrated Budget Risk Management
Quantitative Assets Allocations
Equity Portfolios & Foreign Markets
Numerical Estimating Calibrations

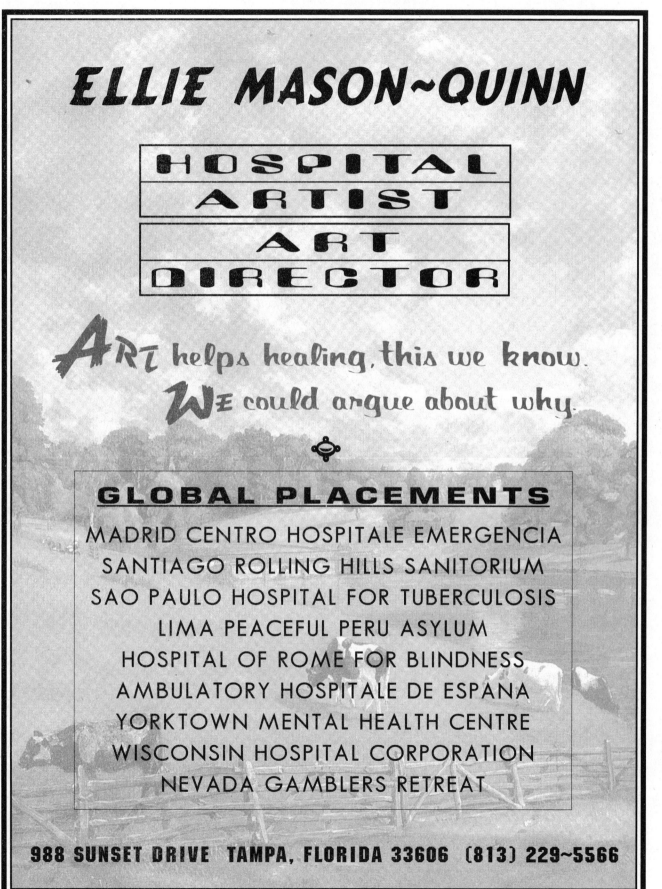

ELLIE MASON~QUINN

HOSPITAL
ARTIST
ART
DIRECTOR

Art helps healing, this we know.
We could argue about why.

GLOBAL PLACEMENTS

MADRID CENTRO HOSPITALE EMERGENCIA
SANTIAGO ROLLING HILLS SANITORIUM
SAO PAULO HOSPITAL FOR TUBERCULOSIS
LIMA PEACEFUL PERU ASYLUM
HOSPITAL OF ROME FOR BLINDNESS
AMBULATORY HOSPITALE DE ESPANA
YORKTOWN MENTAL HEALTH CENTRE
WISCONSIN HOSPITAL CORPORATION
NEVADA GAMBLERS RETREAT

988 SUNSET DRIVE TAMPA, FLORIDA 33606 (813) 229~5566

PLOW TO
REAP TO
SOW TO
REAP TO
PLOW.
KEEP PLOWING.
KEEP PLAYING.

ZurichTelo SSA
Euro$660,000 Cable-Links
Switzerland 2006

SOME FIELDS I HAVE
HARVESTED
LATELY

BellTeleCon Italia
$800,000 Media Blitz
Atlantic Seaboard 2005

Saskawan ASA
$1.5M TV Buy
Soccer Finals 2002
Futball Superdrive 2001

T–Mobilo Europe
$600,000 Ad–Sats (5)
North Euro Inter-Connect
2002 – 2004

MiBella Telco PLC
$320,000 Spots (18)
Olympics & World Cups
1998 – 2001

WALEEN
OFFMANN

Dâdi Simcha Perlmuttâr

56 Saksham Karwal Road ✿ Shivas Kaan 39A2X ✿ India ✿ dadiman@indi.net

Here's the deal:

Former Indian–American (dual passport) patent/licensing attorney turned to L.A. prototype designer from luxury autos to high-end appliances and entertainment modules.

HISTORY — B.A., Communications, Michigan State University. Returned to India to work with DeLORENZO DETROIT LTD. in auto software development operations. Specifically, in addition to legal counsel responsibilities, contributed to the advertising campaigns and joint media-mix co-plans for Porsche–Cobara, Nissan–Dodge and Chevrolet–Hundai.

After founding *autoXtremegods.com*, I created numerous blogs for dealing with many industry-wide problems, often resulting in my being hired as a consultant for exorbitant fees. At my AutoLaunchIndex & Image Services, I have been completely "the man to see" for securing trademarks and prototype license arrangements from Asian companies.

Since 2004, I have worked with Tanaka Nippon America, Mitsubishi Dimensional Modeling, Sumitomo Proto, Toyolla–Damlai, SumoSuto and other foreign entities to meet Red China's voracious appetite for copyright infringements, intellectual product pirating, currency tinkering and other big problems.

I recently completed teaching programs at *Tsinghua University* in Beijing and for the Japan Council on Industry Investments.

The SQUEAKY WHEEL MAY GET THE OIL BUT....... GRINDING GEARS GET THE MOST ATTENTION

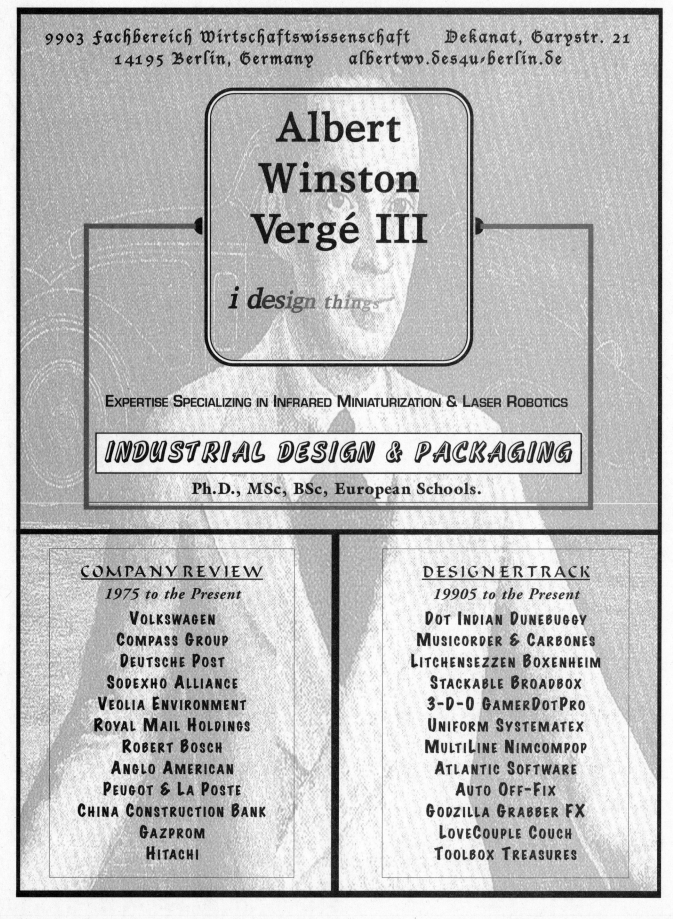

9903 Fachbereich Wirtschaftswissenschaft   Dekanat, Garystr. 21
14195 Berlin, Germany   albertwv.des4u-berlin.de

Albert Winston Vergé III

i design things

EXPERTISE SPECIALIZING IN INFRARED MINIATURIZATION & LASER ROBOTICS

INDUSTRIAL DESIGN & PACKAGING

Ph.D., MSc, BSc, European Schools.

COMPANY REVIEW
1975 to the Present

VOLKSWAGEN
COMPASS GROUP
DEUTSCHE POST
SODEXHO ALLIANCE
VEOLIA ENVIRONMENT
ROYAL MAIL HOLDINGS
ROBERT BOSCH
ANGLO AMERICAN
PEUGOT & LA POSTE
CHINA CONSTRUCTION BANK
GAZPROM
HITACHI

DESIGNER TRACK
1990s to the Present

DOT INDIAN DUNEBUGGY
MUSICORDER & CARBONES
LITCHENSEZZEN BOXENHEIM
STACKABLE BROADBOX
3-D-0 GAMERDOTPRO
UNIFORM SYSTEMATEX
MULTILINE NIMCOMPOP
ATLANTIC SOFTWARE
AUTO OFF-FIX
GODZILLA GRABBER FX
LOVECOUPLE COUCH
TOOLBOX TREASURES

LIFESTYLE PLANNER

A PERSONAL CONCIERGE

WITH A SPECIAL TOUCH

Since 1994, By Land and Sea

AN IMPECCABLE CLIENT LIST

FLUENT ENGLISH & ARABIC

Global Corporated Clients

Diplomat Excelsior Luxury Hotels & Inns

Holland Cruise Lines International

Xerox Europa & Grecian Urn Cruises

Euro Learning Tours International

Spain By Plane & Milennium Vacations

Broken Windows Software Worldwide

Individual Clients

Nathaniel Daniel (Hedge Fund Master)

Melissa Brainard (Genetic Scientist)

Barbie Hopalot (British Pop Star)

Bill E. Woody (Nascar Driver)

Luscious Lovely (Porn Star)

Golong Sabooky (Eastern Philosopher)

Michael Holley Smith (Famous Author)

SERVICES

❀

AIRPORT LIMO BOOKINGS
HOTEL ROOMS
RESTAURANT RESERVATIONS
E-MAIL SERVICE REMINDERS
DE-CLUTTERING SERVICES
ADVANCE OF RELOCATION
PET SITTING & TRANSPORT
MASSAGES & THERAPIES
PEN & BRUSH CLUB EVENTS
RECEPTIONS & GIFTS
HOME & OFFICE DECOR
THEME PARTIES
WARDROBE PARSING

"David has impeccable & superior taste plus a great sense of humor."
— Phillippe Starck
Fashion Maven Extraordinare, Paris

"This man knows lifestyles like the back of his bald head!"
— Opera Diva Fraü Van Schåatten
Berlin Theatre of the Glorious Dead

"Everyone loves this guy. He has been a boatload of monkeys at our most lavish receptions."
— Hotel & Resort Spa Director
The Kempinksi Hotel, Bristol

Jovês Mansala

HOUSE NO. 2, BLOCK 10, STREET 15

KHARTOUM EAST ❧ POB 11270

KHARTOUM ❧ SUDAN

249 183 771474

lifestyledude@sudanman.net

Felipe Zapata

I THINK,
I KNOW.

A Secretary to CEOs & VIPs

PURE CLASS ACT

COMMITTED, QUIET, FRIENDLY, CREATIVE, GOOD HUMORED, PERSISTENT, COOPERATIVE, UNDERSTANDING, PATIENT, ENERGETIC, OPEN-MINDED, HONEST AND MORE.

For a CONFIDENTIAL LIST gladly provided in a personal interview, please contact me at one of the following numbers.

firstratesec@helpmenow.org   class-act-secs@home.com

Days 212-339-7522 OR Messages 338-299-55482

Redwing House
19207 Bluejay Lane
Atlanta, Georgia 39333

JON COCO MONSINI

Home (505) 552-8122
Cell (505) 399-7588
birdhouse@wildseed.net

TRACK RECORD *The Situation Explained*

2001–Present **ARTInFORMS – SAN FRANCISCO & BALTIMORE OFFICES**
SOFTWARE DESIGN PROJECT MARKETING MANAGER

Explained **When I joined this company** it was being managed by a "genius" who had lost all control of the company's most creative innovators, who were by and far the best in their specialty. They were also spoiled and overpaid, having gotten used to performing "at will" and at whatever angle they came up with. The project completely lacked cohesion and direction, which I restored, and brought many of the less glamorized positions (supporting roles) back into the fold.

Results **Market share of VICE VERSA SOFTWARE was <u>improved 38%</u> in 05-06. US Revenues $29M first year & European Licensing $8M first 6-months.**

A MEETING OF MINDS
INVOLVES MORE THAN MINDS MADE UP

Prior to My Current Position

I handled market planning for Wall Street brokerages.
I developed profitable point-of-sale feed-ins for pharmas.
I built national teams to demo surveys for baby-boomers.
I spoke to dozens of groups at seminars & workshops.
I found feasible workthroughs for a hundred problems.
I reported to executives and board members on it all.
I learned how to pry into closed marketplaces.
I taught and mentored my managers well.
I created rewards and incentives that work.
I became known as an "industry best."

BYUNG KWON KIM

A MAN WITH THE **DRIVE** TO GET YOU THERE

DIRECTOR OF SUPPLY CHAIN

MANUFACTURING CONTROL

ENGINEERING & WEAPONS SYSTEMS

2003 TO PRESENT

PIRATI GLOBAL INDUSTRIES

Singapore Office

Instrumental in bringing design-to-prototype phase of various weapons systems into real-time testing and in current deployment overseas. These first-mark products include:

◆ WizKanTractores® Landing Vehicles

◆ SwampMaster® Speedboats

◆ AlqiedaBuster® Sledge-breakers

◆ NightTunnelscope® Infravision

◆ HideyHole® Ditchdiggers

◆ GroovyOvay® Lock-up Attachments

Spearheaded company "Creative 5-Year Plan" initiated in 2003 and tracked progress through all international divisions and foreign subsidiaries. Hired and directed all Singapore staff and set up new manufacturing office in China.

INDUSTRYWIDE EXPERIENCE

Director & Supervising Manager

Project Leading Engineer

Project Creative Director

1988 TO 2003

PIRATI & PRAXMIRE

U.S.A. & Europe Offices

Worked through numerous projects with responsibility for dcsign and development of these highly successful Pirati products used in Indonesia and Thailand:

◆ WideCore® Trackless Vehicles

◆ Coastal Corvette® Patrol Boats

◆ MoonScape® Goggles

◆ ArmorPlus® Protective Vests

◆ VirtuaBlast® Helmets

◆ ImeldaShoe® Combat Boots

FORMAL EDUCATION

Bachelor's degree in Marine Engineering.

TECHNISCHE UNIVERSITÄT DRESDEN

2 Clement Loop No. 03–01   Singapore 629809 Singapore   kim_man@aslaco.sg

PRODUCT DEVELOPMENT

COMMERCIALIZATION

GLOBAL EXPANSION

TELECOMMUNICATIONS

CONSUMER ELECTRONICS

SPORTS & LEISURE

ACQUISITIONS

OUTSOURCING

MARKET STRATEGIES

YAMINA QURINA

Senior Executive

9999 Zentral Strasse
Dusseldorf, Germany
yahwey@dussel.net

MAJOR

TURNAROUND SPECIALIST WHO HAS A TRACK RECORD BEYOND DOUBT

2004–05	MAJOR ELECTRONICS CO.
2001–03	MAJOR APPLIANCE MAKER
1999–01	MAJOR SATELLITE MAKER
1990–95	MAJOR AUTO PARTS MFG.

WHY I SUCCEEDED WHERE

I emphasize control over everything.
I increase stability in management.
I tap into the fear of key managers.
I pose the question: Can you do it?
I bury the "same old thing" quickly.
I unlock the financial puzzle.
I hire multidimensional characters.
I focus entirely on breaking barriers.
I promise exclusive insights for sale.
I am "one of a kind" and proud of it.
I employ subliminal impressions.
I offer stress-free convenience.
I know I can do it, and do it better.
I frequently ask: Am I right for this?
I don't wait for "all the facts" but act.
I spike curiosity and seek happiness.
I don't tell peers & friends everything.
I use silver bullets to hammer points.
I provide all the support asked for.
I do the best because I like to do it.
I also like the comp package with it.

OTHERS BEFORE ME FAILED

I took on the challenges of new concepts that worked so well I have used them quite successfully in businesses for 25+ years.

Lock & Latch Key Company
INTRODUCED STREAMLINED PRODUCT CONTROLS SYSTEMS

Stretto di Messina SSA
REVAMPED CURRENCY EXCHANGE PRACTICES: 18% P/A YIELDS

Sonora Vitacorn (Spiffberger)
COMBINED STAFF FORCES IN M&A TO GAIN 33% MARKET SHARE

Sky & Stone Energy Systems
REFINANCED CAPITAL MARKETING FOR NEW PRODUCT R&D

Yellow Chinese Coal Company
ESTABLISHED COMPANY AS GLOBAL PLAYER VIA PR CAMPAIGN

More Lynch & Deckswab
BROKERED IMPROVED LENDING FOR NEW MFG. PLAN
MERGED SALES & MARKETING FORCES NATIONWIDE

ROBERT Q. RATHBONE

TEAM MASTER
Emerging Technologies
Team Builder Extraordinaire
OUTSOURCING & NETBLOGGING
OFFSHORING & INSOURCING

RECENT ASSIGNMENTS

JAPAN MUSKOGEE CORP.
MANUFACTURING PLANT PLANS

OVERBY WHEATON ILLINOIS INC.
DISTRIBUTION CENTER PLANS
SYSTEM MATRIX DOCUMENTS

ABM/TRICOR WEST CORP.
WAREHOUSING LINKED SYSTEMS
DP CENTERS/INDIA-TO-IRELAND

ACADEMICS

B.A., M.A., MANAGEMENT
University of Wisconsin

CREATIVE MANAGEMENT
Zig Ziglar, Jack Welch, et al.

CONTACT LIST

(938) 662-3486/3488
teambuilder@earthlink.net

Without my help, You just might miss

THE TRAIN

ROMANDO ANTONIO LAMAREZ

Human Resources
Management Pro

Troop Recruiting
Mantime Audits
Mgt. Retransitions
M&A Layering
Key Partner Locks
L-3 Knowledging
In & Out Sources
Info/Commuting
Rapid Resources

27 ROYAL MANOR ROAD
Telephone 800.333.2876

SOUTH PORTLAND, MAINE 04106
roman_go@hrprosnet.com

WILLIAM PRESCOTT MORROW

A MOST EXPERIENCED COUNSELOR

Individuals & Groups
Marriage Arbitration
Divorce Intervention
Crisis Management
Children's Advocate

M.S., COUNSELING
B.S., PSYCHOLOGY
The University of Texas

A Partial List
OF MY LONG-TIME
ASSOCIATIONS

PRESIDIO BAY
PSYCHIATRIC
HOSPITAL

MASSACHUSETTS
MENTAL DEPT.

SAN ANTONIO
ROSE ASYLUMS

SEATTLE—KING
PRIMAL INSTITUTE

401 Elm St. Carlsbad, NM 32282 (393) 335-8944 quig@seekyeme.org

Sassoon Luảm Çang Gai

Chief Conflict Advisor
Chief Technical Advisor

No. 309 Harborplace
Level II – Five Pacific Plaza
88 Queensway Road – Hong Kong
cango@harborlights.org.hk

THE COMPETITION COMMISSION
LONDON BASE
SINCE 1999

Business analyst in Hong Kong operations with a broad portfolio of companies and clients to include banks and financial institutions, global publishing firms, real estate and land developers, large construction companies, health-care and pharmaceutical suppliers/manufacturers.

Before 1999, I attended the University of Hong Kong Business School and received a Bachelor's degree. My career began in earnest at East China Trading Corporation's offices as a market planner; after that I was in charge of container ship & port scheduling for Pacific Seas Shipping Ltd.

Siento Sanchigora

STRATEGY MANAGER

MARKET PROFILES

ASIAN RELATIONS

Boulevard de la Woluwe 56
B-1200 Brussels, Belgium
Tel: (+32-2) 775.98.00
santa@waves.net
sienta@cnook.com

BUSINESS LIAISON

PRODUCT TARGET

ASIAN CONTACTS

Former professor of business and international economic law at the University of Zurich with impeccable academic credentials and language abilities plus fourteen recent years of global business expertise in the US and Asia.

1995-PRESENT   GUARDSMARK GLOBAL SECURITY

Asian Client Liaison – *Critical Component Training*

I've had a lot of other jobs including my professorship but there's nothing like the business of protecting people and corporate assets in our Age of Terror. Not only have I gained experience in such matters as routine loss prevention investigations to dealing with kidnappings and assassinations in distant lands, I offer the wisdom of experience and the ability to manage uncertainty in times of crisis.

My intricate network of global relationships is just an added bonus to hiring me. I'm serious about security. Are you?

MAKE WAVES

before your enemy drowns you

Luiz Lula Ina del Sallo

Calle de los Peritos – Apartado 223

Principali a Castro, Cuidade Montoria

Pays de la Loire Province, New Guinea

10 (22) 3855-6690
dogbark@hounds.org
tailwagsthedog.com

WHOLESALE MERCHANDISING SPECALIST

trilingual
web-based
well-trusted
well-known
world-wise
persistent

THE SHEPHERD
Veterinarian
Vet Products Supplier

proven
popular
informed
net-savvy
forgiving
wide-open

BELIZE □ COLOMBIA □ PANAMA □ ARGENTINA

BARKS & BITES: MY SOUTH-OF-THE-BORDER SALES REPORTS

2005 – Present	Worldwide sales $16M based on net results & foreign currency collections.
2005	WW sales $12M while establishing stronghold in Argentina's metro areas.
2004	WW sales $7.5M and broke into formerly "closed" territories in Argentina.
2002 – 2003	WW sales $6M including first year's web-based sales of over $1.3M net.
2002	WW sales $6M and established subsidiary sales in Europe via Panama co.
2000 – 2001	WW sales $4.8M in South America; $2.6M in Central America.
1995 – 2000	WW sales $2.25M before contracts with Mexico a la Animales in Jalapas.
Prior to 1995	

During the 1970s I was the top salesman for Kimbel Company's pet food products across South America. After accepting an offer from Mars to head up their S.A. and C.A. regional sales operations ("Poco Lobos") I was 1st in sales for 20 years.

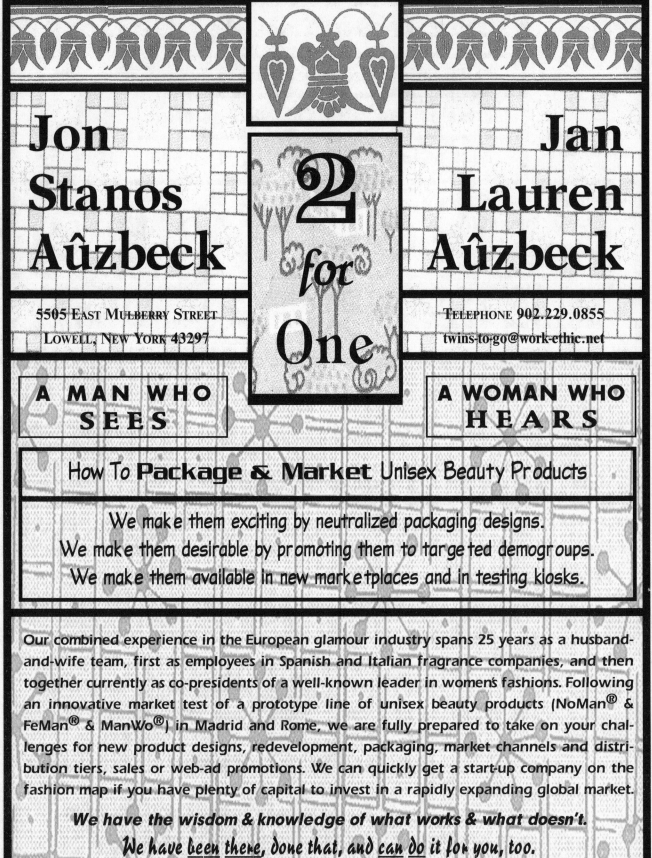

Jon Stanos Aûzbeck

Jan Lauren Aûzbeck

2 for One

5505 East Mulberry Street
Lowell, New York 43297

Telephone 902.229.0855
twins-to-go@work-ethic.net

A MAN WHO SEES

A WOMAN WHO HEARS

How To **Package & Market** Unisex Beauty Products

We make them exciting by neutralized packaging designs.
We make them desirable by promoting them to targeted demogroups.
We make them available in new marketplaces and in testing kiosks.

Our combined experience in the European glamour industry spans 25 years as a husband-and-wife team, first as employees in Spanish and Italian fragrance companies, and then together currently as co-presidents of a well-known leader in women's fashions. Following an innovative market test of a prototype line of unisex beauty products (NoMan® & FeMan® & ManWo®) in Madrid and Rome, we are fully prepared to take on your challenges for new product designs, redevelopment, packaging, market channels and distribution tiers, sales or web-ad promotions. We can quickly get a start-up company on the fashion map if you have plenty of capital to invest in a rapidly expanding global market.

We have the wisdom & knowledge of what works & what doesn't.

We have been there, done that, and can do it for you, too.

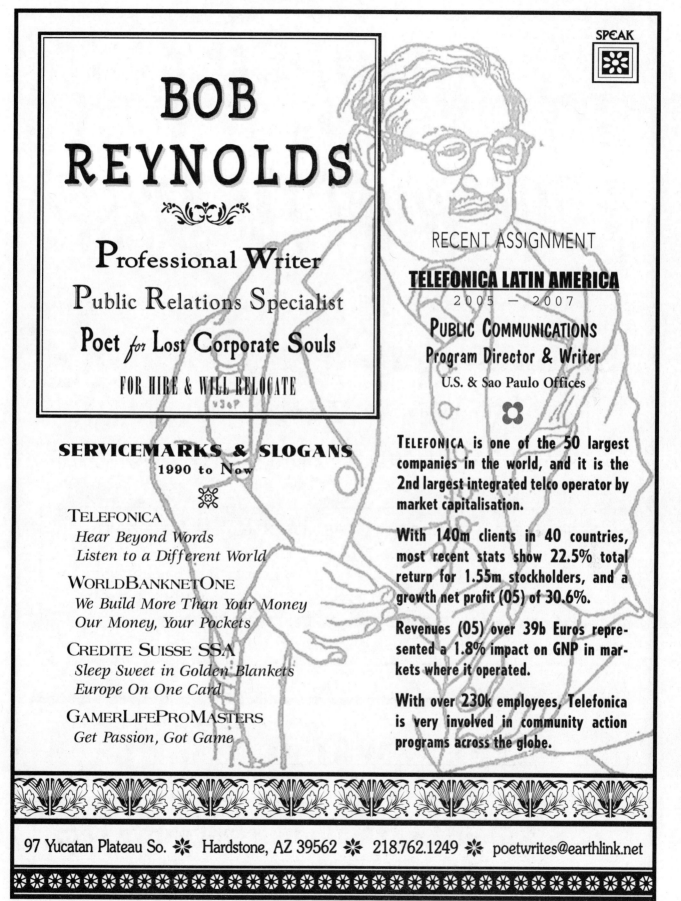

SPEAK

BOB REYNOLDS

Professional **W**riter

Public **R**elations **S**pecialist

Poet *for* **L**ost **C**orporate **S**ouls

FOR HIRE & WILL RELOCATE

SERVICEMARKS & SLOGANS
1990 to Now

TELEFONICA
Hear Beyond Words
Listen to a Different World

WORLDBANKNETONE
We Build More Than Your Money
Our Money, Your Pockets

CREDITE SUISSE SSA
Sleep Sweet in Golden Blankets
Europe On One Card

GAMERLIFEPROMASTERS
Get Passion, Got Game

RECENT ASSIGNMENT

TELEFONICA LATIN AMERICA
2005 — 2007

PUBLIC COMMUNICATIONS
Program Director & Writer
U.S. & Sao Paulo Offices

TELEFONICA is one of the 50 largest companies in the world, and it is the 2nd largest integrated telco operator by market capitalisation.

With 140m clients in 40 countries, most recent stats show 22.5% total return for 1.55m stockholders, and a growth net profit (05) of 30.6%.

Revenues (05) over 39b Euros represented a 1.8% impact on GNP in markets where it operated.

With over 230k employees, Telefonica is very involved in community action programs across the globe.

97 Yucatan Plateau So. ❖ Hardstone, AZ 39562 ❖ 218.762.1249 ❖ poetwrites@earthlink.net

WE AINT ALL THE SAME KNOW WHAT I'M SAYIN?

artist contract management & promotions master

Shaune-X "Lo-Be-Boy" Cartier

THE MAN WITH A MAJOR TALKING PLAN

COMMUNICATING WITH PEOPLE IN A GOOD WAY

DEAF MAN RECORDS   HENDRIX BAY RADIO SHOW
CALIFORNIA FASHION TRAIL   BAYSIDE YACHT SALES
DESERT FLOAT PLANES LTD.   LONDON BRIDGE INC.
MEDIA-HOP TV PRODUCTIONS   LUCY-IN-LOVE LTD.
JIM/JAM JAMBOREE PRODUCTIONS   CAUSEandEFFECT
DOT.DOT INC.   GIMMEGLOBAL CONCERTS LTD.

HERE'S WHERE I'M AT

220 Hillsdale Road   Newark, NJ 08875

888.338.6819   talkin-man@jivealive.com

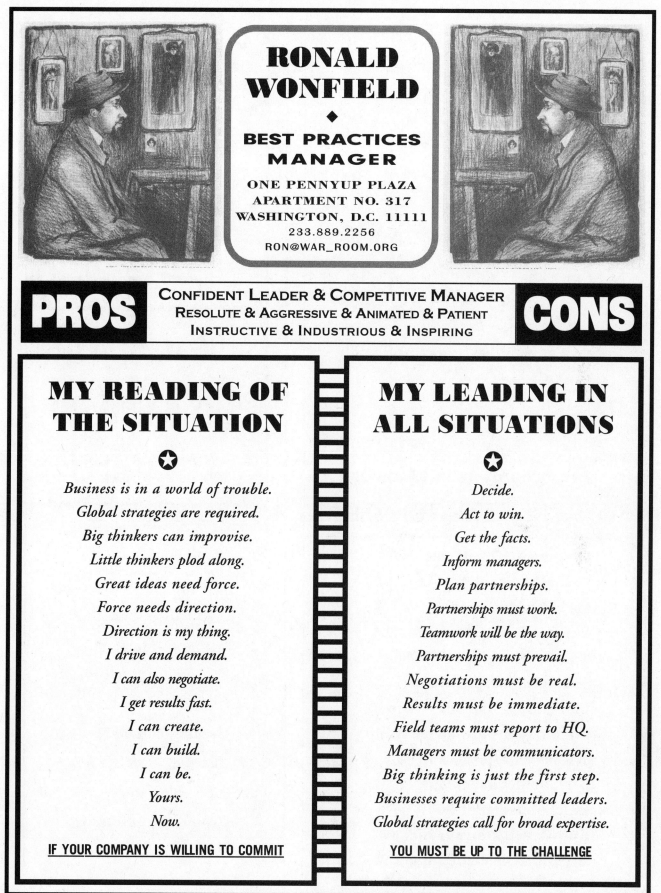

RONALD WONFIELD

◆

BEST PRACTICES MANAGER

ONE PENNYUP PLAZA
APARTMENT NO. 317
WASHINGTON, D.C. 11111
233.889.2256
RON@WAR_ROOM.ORG

PROS

CONFIDENT LEADER & COMPETITIVE MANAGER
RESOLUTE & AGGRESSIVE & ANIMATED & PATIENT
INSTRUCTIVE & INDUSTRIOUS & INSPIRING

CONS

MY READING OF THE SITUATION

★

Business is in a world of trouble.

Global strategies are required.

Big thinkers can improvise.

Little thinkers plod along.

Great ideas need force.

Force needs direction.

Direction is my thing.

I drive and demand.

I can also negotiate.

I get results fast.

I can create.

I can build.

I can be.

Yours.

Now.

IF YOUR COMPANY IS WILLING TO COMMIT

MY LEADING IN ALL SITUATIONS

★

Decide.

Act to win.

Get the facts.

Inform managers.

Plan partnerships.

Partnerships must work.

Teamwork will be the way.

Partnerships must prevail.

Negotiations must be real.

Results must be immediate.

Field teams must report to HQ.

Managers must be communicators.

Big thinking is just the first step.

Businesses require committed leaders.

Global strategies call for broad expertise.

YOU MUST BE UP TO THE CHALLENGE

Hiachi Maguro

28 Avocado Cay
Isla de los Benletti
Palmarona, Italy
theitaliano@manproject.net

the man with his hands on the wheel

Sea & Land Surveys

Eminent Domain

REIT & Trust Accounts

EU Market Caps

Business Modeling

Mediations & Settlements

Legal Research

Mergers & Spinoffs

Foreign Asset Audits

R.E. Tax Issues

Acquisition Matters

Permits & Permissions

An Accomplished Master
MANAGER *of* LARGE PROJECTS

Fantimo & Mohammed (04-08)

Pogoville Saudi Arabia (02-04)

Port Shield–US (04-05)

Defense Battlegroup Ltd. (03)

Ampaq Internationale (01-03)

Southern Energy Starco (99-03)

Chingolia & Sinopec Araco (02)

Pricenstein Watthausen (97, 01)

Wissenschaftszentann (00)

Sozialforschung SSA (95-98)

Reichpietschufer 50 (94-96)

Knowledge Transfer Inc. (91)

Wealthy Fun-deutchland (88)

NOÉMI ZUAZO

INTERNATIONAL MODEL

PARIS
MIAMI
MILAN
TOKYO
VIENNA
MADRID
LONDON
NEW YORK
BARCELONA

GLOBAL ASSIGNMENTS SINCE 1995

Nike
Estee Lauder
PepsiCo
Ferrari Italy
Elant Skies
Sports Illustrated
Land & Polaroid
Proctor & Gamble
Honda Motorcycles
Gelati Skikor
Latin Life Hoy
Calient Amor
Rover Motors
Jaguar
Burma Shave
Tommy Hilfiger
Go Fish!

5'9"   SIZE 6   BUST 35"   WAIST 25"   HIPS 35"
128 LBS.   AUBURN HAIR   MEDIUM COMPLX.   GREEN EYES

SELECTED AWARDS

The Randall Award, *Milan* 2005
The Green Diamond, *Madrid* 2003
The Edgar Snelling Award, *London* 2001
Jacque Denefé Recipient, *Paris* 1998

Miami School of Modeling (4 Years with Madame Dubois Liliac).
Bachelor of Arts, English & Communications (Dual Major/Honors), 1995.
FLORIDA ATLANTIC UNIVERSITY

680 SANDOVAL BOULEVARD W-319   LAGO LAKES, FLORIDA 33356
305.332.5589 OR 305.384.5558 OR NOEMI@TOPNOTCH-MODELS.NET

SAMPLE BIOBLOG #94

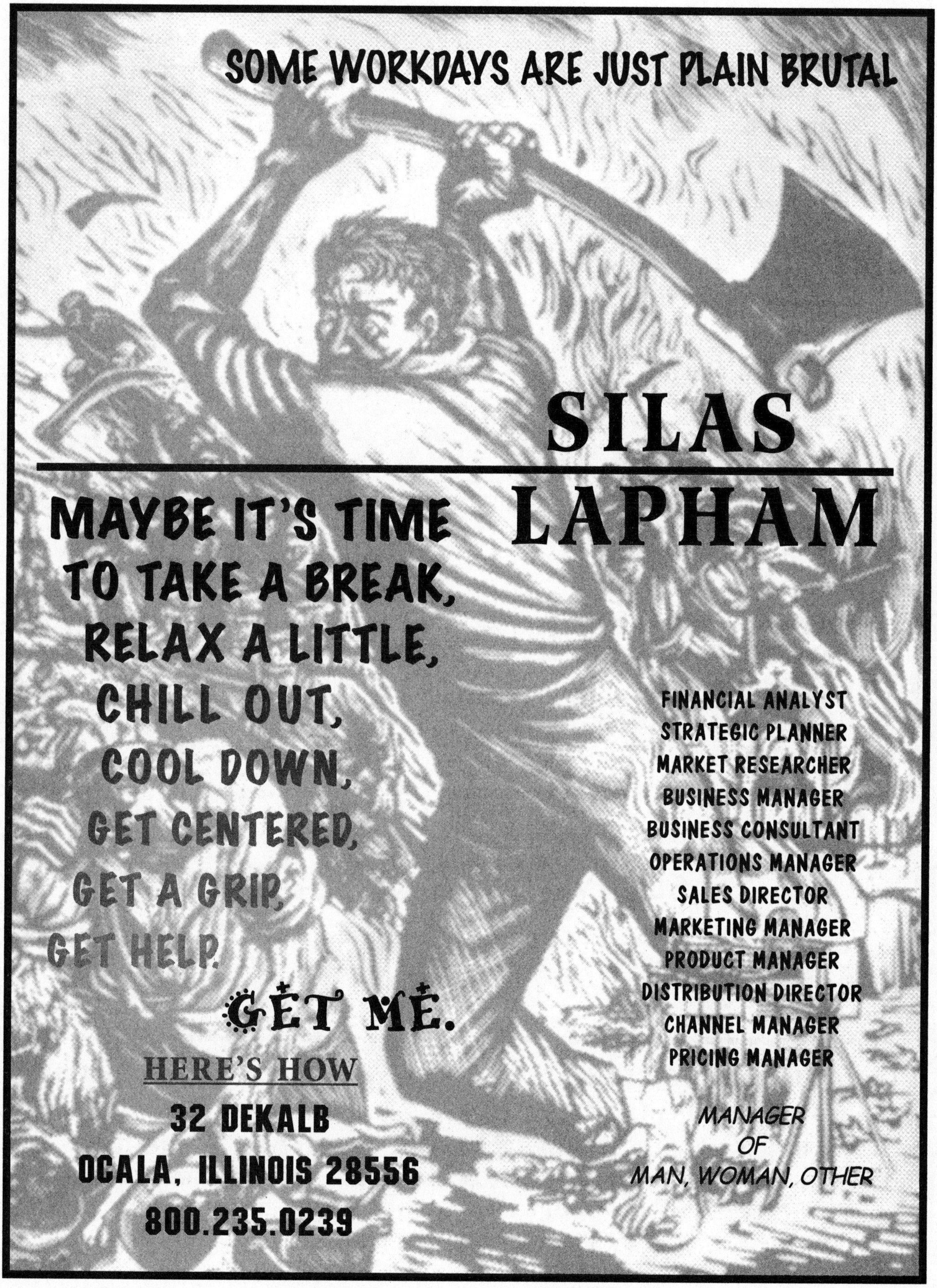

120 Cambridge   Keko, CT 48072   248.345.6683   wie-it@soit.net

MICHELLE WIE

INFORMATION TECHNOLOGIST
DATA & ELECTRONIC COMMERCE
C.A. SOFTWARE TEAM DESIGNER

IT MANAGER BIG 5 CONSULTING FIRM—ERNST & YOUNG, LLP/DETROIT

LAKE ERIE ISAAS E-PROCUREMENT & E-COMMERCE LEADER

BUSINESS PLAN ASSESSMENT & INTERNET SECURITY DIRECTOR

IT STRATEGY & SYSTEMS MULTIPLE INDUSTRIES / DUE DILIGENCE (DOZENS)

FIVE YEARS AT COMPUTER ASSOCIATES DESIGN WORK

B.A., M.A., MATHEMATICS AND SCIENCE, ALBION COLLEGE

ERNEST BLOCK

FARM
TELEVISION
MOGUL

INNOVATOR
── CREATOR ──
MANAGING DIRECTOR

RURAL FARM TELEVISION, INCORPORATED
FOUNDED 2002 — ELK HORN, NEBRASKA

News Bureaus: Chicago; Washington, D.C.; Sao Paolo, Brazil; Monterrey, Mexico.

Parent Company: EchoStar Global Broadcast Communications Corp.

DishSat Network & MultiMediaCom & DirectLatinTV Gropa will be signed and online by 2008.

ENDORSEMENTS

American Angus Association – The Braunvich Association of America

American Maine–Anjou Association – Professional Goat Training Association

National High School Rodeo Association – I Love Alpacas dot.com Association

A LISTING OF MY PROGRAMMING TO DATE

"The Rural America Evening Report"   "Shearing Sheep"

"Farm & Ranch Stock Ticker"   "The Big Palooka Show"   "Rural Farm Heritage"

"Ranchers' Sky Technology Update"   "Farming Global Geopolitics"

"Saturday Night Polkafest"   "The Cattle Auction Show"

"Top Saanen Show Goats"   "Milking Betsy"   "Just Horsing Around"

"Feedlots & Feedbox Fashions"   "Farm & Ranch Lobbies"

RURAL BOX 14   MILLS HILL, NEBRASKA 51991   (545) 329-2266   farmblock@ruraltv.com

LIA ROSANATTI

Is being beautiful still good enough?
No, not in today's organic flower business.

✿

I grew an organic bouquet company in the valleys of California into a major supplier for Earth Foods Internationale (cut flowers from Colombia/Ecuador) including non-pesticide ornamental plants (with Juan Carlos Isaza of Asocoflores & Flor Verde Holland), now encompassing worldwide sales through South American Plant Foundations and Eco-Entrepreneurs Unlimited. Clients include Dole Food Companies, Vacu-Dry of Sebvastopol, Weeden Industries, Newcut Morehouse and other "virgin land" green labels. Worked closely with the the Anglo-Dutch Foundation for Fairness in Flowers and Unilever/Heilmann Tulip Companies.

599 Seaside Lane   Segona Beach, CA 39922   888.222.2988   bloom@floworg.com

Alexander William MacIntosh

CONFLICT STRATEGIST
CORPORATE STORYTELLER
History Buff & LESSON LEARNER

338 Marlboro Lane
Greenville, NC 88334
(350) 522-6686

story-mac@earthwardway.net

2002–Now
BRETON WOODS/MANUFACTURING
Electronic Components/Defense Industry

2000–2002
WARDEN WALKEN MATERIELS LTD.
Merged with Defence Company Great Britain Ltd.
Weapons Components & Transit Tracking Systems

1991–2000
THE ARSELON ARMAMENTS CORPORATION
Weapons & Loading Systems/Transport DP

Ph.D., Philosophy, Yale. Other notable credentials.

We Don't Need To Re-learn Everything

5

HOW TO BUILD A BIOBLOG

BIOBLOGS MERGE BIODATA AND BLOGGING. From our far-flung Internet experience we have inadvertently created a broad unity of vision, expecting to see sophisticated graphics coupled with sensible writing, anticipating meaning in both the underlying visual context of a site and the messages of the accompanying words. Being creative characters, we're also extremely discerning viewers, no longer fooled or easily impressed by splashy visuals or technical prowess. We want to know right up front what's going on, where it's going, what's the point—or we click away forever.

This is why building a bioblog with a sophisticated perspective from conception through execution is so important; it's no time to cut corners. The whole point is to be different and to stand out; originality is integrated into the bioblog to succeed, but employing click art, ready-made, off-the-shelf images, or sloppy writing is tantamount to sabotaging your unique statement and creative effort.

Your concept must be solid and believable, and your self-promotion should be in line with your character. If you are known for your wit and humor, weave it into your overriding concept. If you think of yourself as a deep thinker, hint at that. If you like to shake things up, don't be afraid to lay the foundation. After all, if all works well, at some point you are going to be sitting in the hot seat, explaining to the prospective employer what your bioblog is about—which creative characteristics of the "Great American Combo" menu you have to peddle to them. This is one of the great advantages of your bioblog: it gives you a chance to sketch a personality portrait of your creative character before the employee even has a chance to blink. (A recent *Fortune* article on CEO star power noted that GE's David Calhoun was "a complete package" but that his résumé "can't convey the personal traits that recruiters also salivate over." There's the rub: the better a performer you are, the worse it gets when trying to capture your desirable personal characteristics on a traditional résumé.)

I speak of building a bioblog rather than creating one because it really is like constructing a website made up of two distinct and equal components. And from my perspective, the graphics component carries the load because it says so much more than words can, and, generally, words are the weakest part of résumés regardless of their form because HR people are skeptical of their claims.

In building our bioblog, we already know what we've said in our traditional résumés, and we are going to rework them, slash and slant and stack them in a particular fashion to fit the new image. We will account for the loss of the traditional structure of clumsy categories—job objective, summary, employment history, education, and all of their corrupted cousins—by the commanding presence of your creative character in the visual impact of your bioblog. Thus, the word-work will be easier once we have decided on the image.

IMAGE FIRST

At this point, I can identify five main groups of graphic collections from which you can find a suitable image to build your bioblog, but they by no means represent the limits of available resources. I imagine that once bioblogs are widely distributed by creative workers such as you and your peers, there will be dozens of new categories churned up by biobloggers. For the sake of our first-project exercise, however, here are some places to mine to start with.

1. Old Comics

The ironic humor of old comics puts things into perspective in a way that new ones cannot, and they are a way to catch a reader's eye. Who can resist looking at them? They work to get attention, which is the "best bait" approach you are taking with your bioblog. I suggest the old rule of Keep It Simple, Stupid (KISS) for which images to employ, as a panel or two should be sufficient for your purposes. Be careful not to overplay the irony and humor, but rather to use it subtly to imply that you have a depth of understanding about how things have changed, or how misconceptions about certain workplace topics are often the main obstacle to promoting creativity. The more relevant the panel or subject of it is to your specific target and campaign, the better for you: a sharpened arrow will pierce the armor of even a hardened HR person whose desk is buried in boring résumés. Remember that you are offering your creative characteristics as a partial solution to a prospective employer's "lack of creative people" problem, and you see your wit and humor as part of that fix.

See Sample Bioblogs #3, #8, #33, #34, #38, #41, #45, #67, #82.

2. Old Art

By old art I mean the accepted museum masters, using quickly recognizable images (mostly prints and paintings) commonly found in art books or collection publications, which is where it's easiest to find them for scanning. Using a Degas or Masserl or Renoir will impose an innate and serious authenticity into your bioblog, hooking a reader to ponder it and perhaps wonder what it is about this particular artistic work that you find somehow representative of your creative character.

There has to be a connection in your mind before you can make it believable to a potential employer, especially in a subliminal sense, but that's not hard to do once you come across the image that tugs at your heart or stokes your particular fires. When you find it, you'll know it; you just have to figure out how to use it, lining up the subtle statements of the work with the merits of your creative character and hands-on experience. It's not like you're saying, "Hey, hire me, I could be a Picasso," but more like, "Hello, have you thought about hiring someone who has a heightened sensibility and creative depth for the job?"

If it is relevant as an image that meets your standards and conveys a sense of your worldview, then you can count on it being a reliable vehicle for carrying your message.

See Sample Bioblogs #2, #10, #18, #27, #32, #36, #48, #57, #71, #92.

3. New Art

By new art I mean "modern art," including all the schools and wayward artists on the fringes, from Duchamp and Warhol to performance artists to all those in between. The work will have to be credible enough for you to find it published somewhere (so you can scan it), but it doesn't have to be a Soho gallery piece to suit your purposes; but that being said, again, no cheap shots—it has to possess some obvious aspects of thoughtful consideration and intent of purpose that matches up with your target—and you. You are still the message, a work in progress, and your bioblog can draw upon any art from any source as long as you and your message are joined by a striking image, captivating phrases, and a sensible, believable statement of creative self.

See Sample Bioblogs #11, #14, #35, #54, #58, #72, #77, #89, #94, #99.

4. Photographs

Photographs represent images of real life, and that establishes a first-impression mood of credibility. The reader has to believe the picture, if nothing else, and you can take advantage of that by jumping from that acceptance to your personal statement.

Black-and-white photos impose a force of elemental certainty onto the core of your bioblog, from which you can imply your creative sense of perspective. What HR person could not take a fleeting moment to study a great photo? What HR person would not find this a welcome break from the ocean of "coordinated" and "increased sales" and other detached phrases of traditional résumés. This is advertising, and we're all hooked. Catch the HR rep off guard, before he blinks, and make your best case while he's wondering, What's this? Who's this?

Photographs offer the broadest realm of available images; you could conceivably even use your own works: self-portraits, anonymous workplace shots, curious human dynamics in play—whatever you want to ride on with your message of creativity. You could develop specific images for a variety of slanted bioblogs for a spectrum of prospective employers, increasing your arsenal with highly defined bioblogs designed for different types of companies, much like traditional résumés employ optional "objectives" for multiple purposes.

An example of the obvious would be to use a stock photo of Charlie Chaplin caught up in the grinding gears of a machine, coupling that with your bioblog's promoting your ability to prevent employees from being overwhelmed by management's decisions: let the photo create the ambience for your words.

Many times these image–word relationships are simple sets: a hard work image coupled with words depicting determination (leadership characteristics), etc. If you want to get a head start on your image search, choose a couple of the creative characteristics from "Great Character Combos from the American Workplace Menu" (pages 26–29)—such as resourceful and tenacious—to determine the parameters for your image search.

See Sample Bioblogs #60, #69, #79.

5. Altered Media

Collages and advertising media, altered by the hand of an artist, can render a powerfully subtle background message that can support your argument for your creative prowess. Try it if this is something you are comfortable with, because you are sure to be noticed for your originality. It takes more work, but the images are truly curious to the eye.

Media such as print ads or newspaper copy can be used effectively, or even the images found on money and other formal documents. A child's watercolor, magazine covers, posters, commercial art, Chinese drawings, or an old letter can provide the right mood. The general mood established by these graphics is a quiet foundation for the weightier word; these are supportive images, not domineering ones, that make up a personal wallpaper on which you can post your words. Better yet, these images require only a minimal amount of relevancy, and they can be used simply to spice up the otherwise lacking bioblog. In addition, they can be combined with major message-carrying images as secondary, backup graphics for fill and emphasis.

See Sample Bioblogs #4, #13, #23, #26, #42, #49, #51, #64.

WEIGHTED WORDS

The biggest problem with traditional résumés is their complete and total reliance on the strength and effect of words, which, due to the millions of résumés in daily distribution, have become so weakened and diminished by monotonous use that they simply can't carry the water anymore. Fortunately, our brains still respond automatically (often instinctively) to a provocative image, so as far as words go on bioblogs, they need to be short and sweet, a respite for the weary HR person. In a bioblog, the value of relying on the image for content is to take the load off words.

Let's start with some plain and simple truths, some rules of the road we can agree on that support our bioblogging:

1. You're just trying to get in the employer's door for a personal interview.
2. Hopefully, the HR person will appreciate your originality.
3. If you do it well, that HR person will also understand your message.
4. Your message is carried first by the force of the image/graphics.
5. Your words must not detract from that effect, but add to it.
6. Your words need to display your track record, but in a creative way.
7. Your creative character is what you are offering, not a work history.

With these tenets understood, handling your message will be a matter of taking your old résumé and revamping it to (1) express yourself first and foremost *as a creative person,* (2) generate interest in the portrayal of your past, which should (3) indicate a sense of direction for your (creative) future. You don't want to tell the HR rep everything, and she doesn't want to hear all of it. Don't be afraid to build from the premise that "this is about me, not where I've been." The best way to understand what I'm referring to is to peruse the hundred sample bioblogs and note the countless approaches to reporting achievements, experience, education, and other typical résumé data sets.

The main rules of the road for bioblogging are those of good taste and sensible design, and what you do depends on who you are, how creative you want to be, and where you want to go. The following section offers two step-by-step examples of building a bioblog, one for a man and one for a woman, which I hope will be sufficient for you to understand how to go about tackling your own.

BIOBLOGGING #1

Let's take a man who has three decades of experience under his belt, and he's been involved in the marketing side of product development long enough to recall in painful detail how everything used to be done differently. To some job seekers in his shoes, being "old enough to remember" would be a liability that would have to be hidden or downplayed in a job market that no longer appreciates old pros. He's got a problem to deal with, and in traditional résumés, there's no place to hide: to be credible they practically *require* a seamless career path of related jobs and titles without so much as a break (as unrealistic as that is).

Our candidate's problem is that his creativity—thereby, his ultimate and future value to a new employer—is inextricably woven into his considerable experience: viz, he wouldn't know what he knows if he hadn't been around long enough to learn it. The curse of wisdom, perhaps, but he has a plot, which is to play to his audience with his supposed weakness. Rather than try to gauze over his age/experience and the assorted past employers (good and bad), he can take a straight-on approach and build his bioblog around the image of "old." Thus, he chooses the plate below.

This image brings subtle information with it: the old days of hard work, focus, and concentration, pleasure of teamwork, busy taskers making progress, review and acceptance, cooperation, expertise, apprenticeship, defined duties and more—all good and positive aspects of a well-functioning workplace whenever and wherever it is. These are aspects, in fact, that drive most successful businesses.

Next, he decides what he wants to say, or what he would like to say if he could have five minutes alone with somebody important in the company he wants to work for, and that is:

I know what hard work and cooperation can do.
Because I earned that knowledge the old way.

He knows that if they are determined to hire a "youngblood," it will make no difference what he did or has learned, but if they are open to a creative approach to the position they are trying to fill, they may give him a shot at it. It may, in fact, be up to him to get them to think about the position in a new way, such as, What could a really innovative person do with these responsibilities, on this particular team? Are we perhaps looking for the same qualities that ended up badly last time?

But there's more to the story: our candidate has truly notable accomplishments that get lost in his résumé when declared like all the other elements of his "employment record" and "work experience." Like all of us, his particular strengths and/or abilities are relative to the situations in which they played out. The courage upon which a creative commitment has been taken at work is often overlooked both at the workplace and in the traditional résumé, for, in reality, taking a creative risk at work can be a major career risk as well.

Eventually, if you want to move up, you have to put your money where your mouth is, even if it leaves a bad taste. We all know that our creative characters at work do not function in a vacuum, so we are faced with a situation where trying to get a complete stranger (the mysteriously unknowable HR person out there somewhere) to understand the significance of our role in a specific event (in one of millions of variant workplaces) cannot be helped by utilizing a well-worn, relatively outdated model of a résumé—the traditional achievements section of a résumé, so often suspiciously doctored, embellished, pumped up, and selectively edited. In other words, does anybody believe any of the words anymore?

Your bioblog offers you a viable alternative: make your creative impact, the positive and intriguing first impression, before the HR rep has a chance to blink, with the zap and zing of a first-response image. What's this? is what you want your reader to think before getting into the context of your words. "What's this about, and who is this person?" is the desired progression. In light of this strategy, having chosen a stiff and staid image on which to base the textual content, our candidate will distill the obligatory content of chronology and credentials down to the same kind of sharp-edged, keen-cutting, shotgun-blast meaning with a capital *M* that is accomplished with a succinct image.

He will take the mundane duties and responsibilities written into his routine roles in market research, advertising, promotion, and marketing/sales management and perform a major lobotomy on its public personality. Rather than replay the corporate job descriptions, he will transform the faceless, standard operating phrases of "investigated," "analyzed," "coordinated," and "successfully organized" into personal terms pointing to him—his particular workplace menu of personality traits and creative characteristics. It is a matter of converting impersonal action verbs that seem to require no direct owner (not "I coordinated" by forcing everyone on the sales staff to be accountable, finally, for once, but "coordinated" like an automaton) and letting the real reason for success—the candidate behind the bioblog—get masked over by the redundant words.

Having chosen a medieval image of "a day at the office," which has the dust of humor on it when contrasted to today's highly computerized work environments, he establishes an image of "old" for a basic workover. By superimposing onto this image some well-edited text, as a media ad might employ, he introduces a new layer of meaning and depth to his bioblog, and it starts to get personal. It not only carries a tone of revolutionary zeal (thereby, a *youthful* spirit), but it brings up the essential topic of brands, which have been around a long time if one thinks about it—the realm of his special expertise. He has surprised the reader by making a powerful and striking statement of what he has learned about marketing brands, and that packaging that is too clever often fails, which costs a company money and lost opportunities.

Knowing *what not to do* is as important as *what to do,* and is part of his overall qualifications. But this enterprise of bioblogging is about him, not his history, and he won't skirt the fact that he is the engine behind all this. *I can, I will, I am, I did* is the real progression that is relevant to his target—to all of our targets!—and to the company that will foot his future bill. Employers are learning that the past is increasingly irrelevant.

By avoiding nondescript and hackneyed action words that point to no one, and instead directing all text toward his own menu of creative characteristics, he plays his royal flush to the house, the employer: *Here's what I have—not where I've been.*

The next step:

Here's the traditional executive summary that would be used by a regular résumé for this man: *Marketing executive with over twenty years experience in sales and marketing management; excellent reputation as a creative, innovative manager capable of successfully revitalizing old product lines and introducing new; full range of marketing and sales experience to include market research, market planning and analysis, advertising and promotion, sales and sales management.*

Boy, does that sound exciting or what? Makes you want to grab a phone and call this guy in for an interview, right? Not likely. This is boilerplate drivel and says nothing about who this man is and what he has the potential to do to improve the lot of a company looking for someone like him—even if it doesn't yet know it. So our man takes a strong (risky) position in his bioblog:

That's his new executive summary from his product branding and market experience; this is what he's learned whether it crystallized the first day he landed a job in product research and marketing, or if it took twenty years to figure it out as the global marketplace turned into a fragmented world of niches and products. It doesn't matter when he gained the expertise and perspective to see through obstacles, it's the fact that he has learned the simple truth of success in his trade: *Know your competitors well, but know your own products better.* His philosophy is wrapped in the package of his creativity.

To crank it up a notch, he will choose a secondary but equally visually powerful image as the foundation for the knockout punch—the second message level. For this, he chooses a striking woodcut of a Parisian street scene of a confrontation between the archetypical bourgeois boss and the restless worker-masses, an image that is loaded to the hilt with subliminal context and prerevolutionary zeal, and adds to his statement the implication that walls must be broken down to make an impact.

His bioblog has begun to take shape—*it has a look.*

He's made his simply stated business philosophy with a straightforward graphic and a dozen words. An HR person is very likely to find this intriguing and curiously familiar (because it looks like an ad). Instead of having to plow through

Marketing To Picky People Is Not For Sissies.

The Risks Are Big.
The Rewards Are Fleeting.
It Takes Initiative.

It's what I do.

the typically unremarkable list of "distinctions" that occupy the surface of most résumés when trying to "read" the personality of this candidate rendered by his bioblog, the HR person will quickly get an idea of the way he thinks and, by extension, the way he operates in the workplace. He's said something significant in his résumé, rather than report indiscriminate job-related facts. This is *new*.

Our candidate could stop here and choose to list whatever particular dates, names of companies, titles, etc., he feels obliged to in order to make the cut for the targeted companies, and he can very well create a store of various versions for forthcoming needs. He could also take a creative leap for maximum shock effect in a situation that he feels is so extremely competitive that he should go all out.

He has now packed his bioblog full of context and content, like an old leather trunk pasted over with decals from a dozen around-the-world cruises, exhibiting a "been there, done that" presence and sensibility. To be sure, this is the résumé of a man who is self-confident, who knows what he's talking about, and it shouldn't really matter if it took ten or thirty years to get to this point. The dirty little secret is, he wouldn't be willing to stick his creative neck out if he wasn't sure what he's worth in today's market. Where he learned it is important and germane to any prospective employer, and that data will certainly be revealed sooner or later if it isn't already on the bioblog, but more paramount are the issues and matters of what, not the record of when or where.

Bioblogs are about the future you, not the "I did this or that" of traditional résumés. If I seem to reiterate this particular point, thus becoming tiresome by redundancy, please forgive me, but this is a point that needs to be driven home more than once. Don't forget how user-unfriendly résumés evolved over the years, effectively banning the "I" altogether, as if action verbs need no owner, no prime mover. Everything just happened and, by inference, to some degree through the efforts of the person who owned the résumé, but everyone began to look too similar for their liking. Bioblogs bring the "I" back in a big way, and it's important to keep that view fresh in your mind when constructing the visual framework of your bioblog: it's about you, and that's okay.

Mr. Chamberlink's bioblog simply oozes with expertise, and there is no better way to sum up the hands-on decisions and judgment making entailed in his work history, for, to be truthful, it would take a twenty-page essay to explain the unique marketplace challenges and corporate restraints of all the business activities, at each and every employer, for all the teams and ideas and market changes he has worked his way through day by day, year by year, decade by decade.

The job of his bioblog is to grab a reader's attention, and then flash a message across the open window in the nanosecond the reader is likely to give it. There's just no way he can point to his expertise other than to throw it up on the screen and see it stick. From the visual imagery of his bioblog, do we really care how old he is, or how many companies he's worked for, or what specific products he's worked into the mainstream?

For our sample's final version, we'll go ahead and plug in the routine data sets that are generally required by HR people so you'll know how it can be placed into the overall graphics layout, edited down to the bare-bones skeleton of chronological history and academic status. There are so many disparate companies and changing versions of titles across the broad American business plains that few of them stand out, and there is no valid reason to go into any detail at this point in the job-seeking process. The one thing that hasn't changed since the 1940s and that bioblogs still share with traditional résumés is this: they're still just bait, and you should not tell the whole story on your résumé.

Remember, your bioblog is designed to secure an interview, and that's all. After that it's all in your court, the responsibility to make sense of what you have claimed to be truly representative of the creative character you possess, and the benefits of your potential to the company you are targeting.

Let's see what the two images combined and the addition of highly edited textual content add up to for our sample.

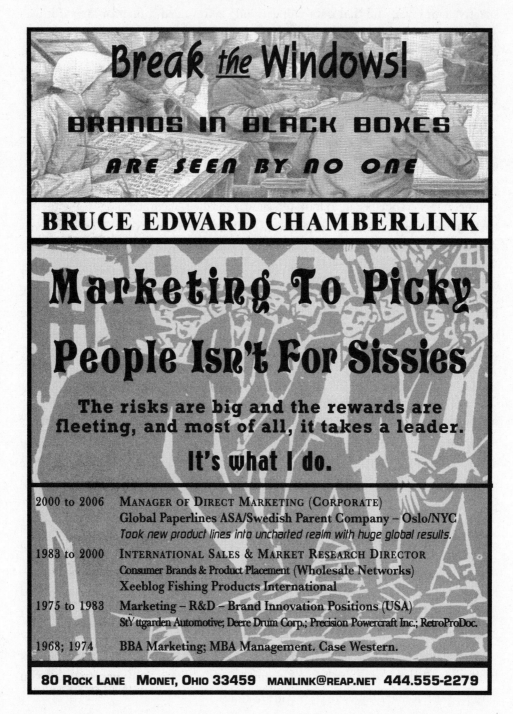

Let's take a look at building a bioblog for a woman with fifteen years in the retail business, one of those tough markets where creativity can count for a lot and make a big difference in results. Like many people in her trade, she has worked her way up the ranks from her first job as a store's clerk and stocker, having learned the ropes of markdowns and seasonal inventories, as well as what kind of advertising campaigns worked and what didn't. She's got a long career ahead of her, but she wants to fast-track into high pay, and she's convinced that it is her creativity that can be the vehicle to the salary base she's aiming to achieve.

Ah, but there's more! These fifteen years occurred before she spent seven years in advertising as a broadcast buyer and spot account manager (which happened, like many job opportunities, when she met a resourceful senior executive at a social event); so, she has a couple of things to deal with—explaining the misunderstood and negative disconnect between her two careers (now media, but used to be retail), and converting the advertising background into viable, supportive credentials for her primary target: a high-paid retail management job.

These two dynamics are brought easily into convergence with the cross platform of the graphically competent bioblog. The most obvious device, to me, would be to play upon the singularity of her experience as unique and qualifying, since both fields are on the same stage of worldwide product competition. Effective imagery is essential in both of her experience data sets and is a logical mainstay for her bioblog. The words that drag out the routine stuff of retail and media buying certainly won't, per se, bring any pizzazz into her pitch. It's got to be a visually stunning bioblog in order to get them to do what any bioblog is aimed to do, getting them first to look, then to listen.

As a professional, with considerable retail coordinating in her bag, she can claim certain core strengths as facets of her creativity: knowledge of the best methods for keeping up with trends in a timely fashion; a well-developed sense of forecasting surges in demographic buying patterns (e.g., preteens); discovery of effective avenues for moving overshadowed lines back into brand limelight; the big-picture focus requisite in developing strategic corporate and innovative relationships with suppliers and vendors; a natural ability (from her creative menu) for nurturing relationships into improved profit margins; and hard-core experience in crunching numbers with financials based on real net nets.

The trick is, whether it's for a designer collection or a diffusion line, for footwear and handbags or spot ads for spirits—she has learned that a team leader is (1) someone who knows the shortest route from Unknown to Well Known, and

(2) someone who can take skeptics under her wing and convince them to commit fully to propelling a business plan into best practices.

It just so happens that this is the link that connects the dots in her background: whether it was placing broadcast time for MasterCard in Minneapolis or Orion in Omaha, she knew what the real effect was supposed to be, the measurables; and when she made over low-performing departments in major shopping malls, she knew where the bar was set, and reached it.

She's a high performer whose creativity is more subtle than those around her realize because she's not flamboyant, no corporate starlet sucking up all the air in a room. What she can do is pick up with her "sixth sense" what it will take to get a sales team revved up to maximum speed and heading in the right direction. Her emotional intelligence works best when clearing the obstacles in the path of her team, the individual workers who own their own toolboxes of skills and creative characteristics. In the old days of traditional résumés, she would be called a "shirt-sleeve manager" who "works well under pressure" or worse, is a "people-oriented" person. (Ha!)

What she has really learned from the two experiences, media and retail, is that advertising ultimately is targeted at an individual's intelligence, or innate sense of self-consciousness—be it via humor or contrast or whatever mode—and that an ad concept succeeds only if it makes a lasting impression on a person's mind as it might relate to him and his own creative experience.

Selling (retail) and buying (media space) are like cops and robbers; they need each other. Finding the right place and time for a Supercuts spiel or a Payless Shoe-Source promotion is knowledge worth knowing; and it can gel with experience in Eddie Bauer and Elizabeth Arden. Or at least in her mind, it can; but how does she formulate an argument based on an image and the rhetoric of words?

This is her big problem, getting around the HR person's knee-jerk reaction to the fact that she is currently in media, not retail, where she wants to be moved to the front of the line, for they are likely to think of this as a liability, like some prison term that must be buried under a sabbatical. Her first task is, of course, to get their attention; the next step has to be to convince them that she knows exactly what she is offering, and that she has nothing to hide. She'll do the work for them, making the media jobs of value to the retail experience; and if they can't think "out of the box," she will give them instructions.

She has to begin with a strong image statement, for sure; then she can decide on what the text is going to say in order to sustain the "argument" of the image—i.e., she wants to be taken seriously and in a positive light. She needs to disarm the view that the two careers are incompatible, then show the HR person these careers are mutually supportive; and she needs to show that she isn't stuck, that she is appropriately prepared for prime time retail responsibilities.

Her bioblog must show that while she may be different, that doesn't mean that she is less qualified than people with twenty-two years all in the same retail zone. Most of all, she knows her bioblog has to get her foot in the door so she can sell herself in person, which is her forte and which she has done many times. She knows that mere words in the traditional résumé format didn't cut the mustard then and won't now. She needs a bioblog that is a marvelous doozie!

She has done a lot of research into "feminine" images and has lined up three possibilities for a graphic approach to her chronology problem. Now she must evaluate those three for their individual pros and cons if utilized in her comprehensive campaign that will center around her bioblog.

Here are her three options for a dominant image:

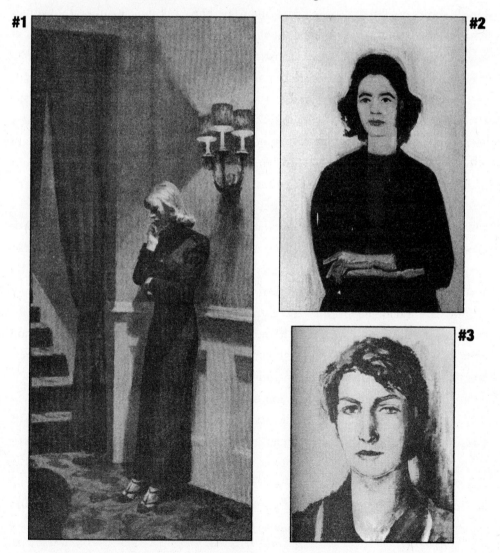

She believes that each of these is fairly reflective of her creative character, since they all register an air of clarity, substance, and self-possession. The operative point of view that prevails in #1 is one of pensive contemplation (Edward Hopper's painting of a woman listening to concert music), and is symbolic to our candidate of the depth of her resourcefulness, as well as her ability to think through the problems that make others (less valuable others) stumble and fail. The image is especially appealing to her because it happens to signal one of her favorite subjects—acting (she can see retail as a form of absurd theater)—but the most pressing facet on its behalf is the subtle stairway in the painting's background. She sees it as a representation of the career path at the end of her rainbow—or in front of the gate she must first open. The thoughtful pose of the woman's pondering predates her choice to put herself in the bioblog and onto the employer's table.

Image #2 is less informative, safer, more like a photo attached to an actor's bio. It shows a calm and collected woman, perhaps a manager unlike the women who run the fashion departments: she's one of us, and thus, one of them, easy to relate to, which is a valuable characteristic from the "Great Character Combos." But there's no edge to this image; it's too quiet, not ambitious enough, not openly ready to climb through the bramble patch to get to the finish line. Our candidate isn't looking for a nice fit; she's searching for a chance to take charge of a company's meat-and-potatoes operations and institute changes to make it work, and to make people want to change to get there. There's not enough drive and activity lurking in the subliminal background of this image, so out it goes.

Image #3 contains a little more determination and self-assurance, and whereas the previous one gazed a bit off past the eye of the camera (a composed, television type of stance), this one is a stare down: unflinching, constant, maybe more independent than the others: not particularly young, but old enough to have been on the front lines for some credible amount of time, a tour of duty that can be chronicled or not with a detailed chronology. As much as she is attracted to this image of a woman who is at peace with herself and willing to make direct contact—especially with a stranger in the HR office—she falls back to the mood and tone of Hopper's woman, which is decidedly serious and self-conscious.

She thought it over, decided, and here it is.

She's determined that her bioblog will be structured around two blended motifs: *contemplation of decision making* (in business, aka calculation and planning) and *career phases* (the personal steps that we all must walk through to go somewhere). And because the physical dimensions of the image #1 are tall and deep, she will take the opportunity to build the bioblog in two parallel parts—left side image, right side words—whose carefully crafted components will bounce off one another like beams on a diamond.

This parallel arrangement is a useful format for bioblogging because it makes editing the text according to the space available easy; moreover, it allows the option to superimpose additional text onto the image itself—sometimes wise, sometimes not, depending upon whether it creates unnecessary clutter. I prefer a clean image when possible after carefully choosing one that needs no additional work to establish its value. However, not all images are from the hands of a modern master, so you may choose to paste on some type to give it more punch, or simply to distract from something in the graphic that isn't appropriate for your purpose.

Okay, our candidate has decided on her public persona: meditative, not capricious, a thinker—a complete woman in a woman's trade. She has a few major "word categories" to nail down:

1. her unique and self-vetting *statement of creative self*
2. her *purpose*: what the bioblog is all about
3. her disjointed career record (she'll have to get it out front ASAP)
4. her track record redirected toward her *future value*
5. her other credentials: from peers, training, personal experience

Combining all of the above with the powerful presence of her underlying creative personality traits will give her a powerful bioblog to persuasively sell the product of her natural self and the complexities of her creative experience in the business worlds of retail and advertising. She may have to figure out a way to connect her media work with Clorox to retailing Liz Claiborne, or translate BellSouth experience to bikinis, but the overarching effect should be to raise the eyebrows of that HR person on the other end who comes across this newfangled résumé and thinks, Well now, what have we here? Looks like somebody worth talking to, someone who has more to reveal if you want to dig deeper into what they think they are capable of.

Employers are looking for those creative people who can merge their left-brain insights with their right-brain know-how: those spirited, compassionate, clear-thinking, practical-minded team leaders who can bring their staffs to share in the process of completing successful projects and moving the company forward, who add both velocity and gravity to the equation of teamwork.

Since employers hire creative character and not skill sets, she can campaign actively as having worked on both sides of the dollar: selling the image that brings in the buyer, and shaping the product to match the preferences (and peculiarities, at times) of the buyers. The marketing psychology crosses the invisible border of seller versus buyer, and our candidate's creative spark is in making the big-sweep focus align with the budget and projections. This is no small matter.

Only her words can make this point well. The image will lay the groundwork and break the ice, but those few words she chooses must be as strong as a header over a window; otherwise, the whole house may collapse. The bioblog could buckle from overselling if she's not careful, so she will trim to the bone everything she says. The image is heavy enough without a lengthy executive summary or laborious work history and assorted claims of accomplishments.

Let's see what it looks like now with the two parallel elements joined.

What has she done to make her case? First, she's established herself as a woman and as a thinking one at that. This is carved in stone. One can only start from the initial impression that she has given a lot of thought to this business of promoting herself—her creativity—and it's unlikely that an HR person has come across a résumé that is this compelling before. The image works: it not only rings true, but it plants a seed of interest almost immediately. *What's this? Who's this? What's she doing? What's she want? What are those stairs leading to?*

Before the blink.

In the rapid flash of recognition, the reader's eyes wander to the banner heading: VAGABONDS OF VOGUE. What are they? Where is this going? One has to plunge into the text to find the clues, and this is where the statement truly begins to materialize: it's about retail management, typically a jejune topic that doesn't spark much curiosity.

She chooses a single paragraph to encapsulate her media-cum-retail philosophy: design to win. In less than a hundred words, she has connected the two islands of her career's geography: the media-buying jaunt and the longer-term retail track. It begins to make sense, the two together, considering how in business they are as likely a couple as the horse and buggy. Succinctly and straight to the point, she has dismantled the potential negative arguments that an HR person might make against her: that she hasn't been exactly on the right course, that she might have wasted her time. She skillfully makes the media work speak for itself for what it was.

Next, after dressing up the showcase with some ornamental jewels, she uses just nineteen words to establish her professional competence level, the turf where she feels most confident and comfortable. This is high-end and high-yield territory, warranting high pay. She makes no claims about sales percentages or the routine drivel of sales and marketing résumés; she knows she can pull up the charts and portfolio later, in person; and she knows her essential mission right here—before the blink—is to fill the void with positives on her behalf: a strong woman image *plus* a smart and savvy marketing executive. This approach to detailing her creativity rather than describing the dates and places and titles she has in her collected baggage serves the consummate purpose of keeping the attention focused on her future worth, not her former workplaces, the occupied land of 95 percent of traditional résumés.

This is what the HR person wants a glimpse of.

This is tribal marketing of a breakthrough brand—her creative self.

This is retail advertising of one's creative self at its best.

This is bioblogging.

JOSEPHINE HARRISON

❦

VAGABONDS OF VOGUE

The business of retail management is akin to the cat chasing its tail: What do you do when you catch it? How do you know when to abandon trends and go with your instinct? How do you position a family of multi-line brands in the price wars of megasellers and deep discounting? In today's advertising, losing momentum is a death spiral; in retail, it's a funeral. You can't allow your merchandisers to wander like vagabonds in vogue, hoping for a handout from a compassionate Calvin Klein. You can succeed only with a winning design.

✺ ✺ ✺

**DASHBOARD REAL-TIME REPORTING
PRODUCT SOURCING TURNOVERS
MERCHANT NEGOTIATIONS/RELATIONS
VALUE PACKAGING & CELEB TIE-INS
I.T. INVENTORY CYCLING/CONSUMER
RESEARCH & GRASSROOT CHANNELS**

Truth In Art – Media Is Run By Retail

RETAIL IN THE FOREGROUND
MISS MARCY APPARELS: Merchandising VP & roll-out specialist for 17 product lines (MVP 1 year; others 4 years). GREAT OUTDOOR CLOTHING CO. Distribution & Inventory Control Manager (4 years). ZIGGY FABRICANO FASHIONS: Marketing Coordinator/Buyer (6 years).

MEDIA BUYING IN THE BACKGROUND
BUNG & RUBLE: Senior Spot Buyer ($15m p.a. 5 years) for major global tv and print accounts: Visanet, Gillette, Verizon, Wilson, Yahoo, Henley, Fordham, Plush, Frenetic Toys, Intrepid, Givenchy, Martha Stewart, Revolvo, Desparté, Jaguaro and Latin American cos.